THE COMPLETE
MEDITERRANEAN DIET COOKBOOK
FOR BEGINNERS

2000+ Days of Simple and Easy Recipes to Boost Your Health and Promote Weight Loss with a 28-Day Meal Plan, Personalized Health Journal, Shopping Lists, and Budget-Friendly Recipes for Every Day

CHAPTER 3:
APPETIZERS AND SNACKS

CHAPTER 4:
SALADS AND SIDES

CHAPTER 5:
SOUPS AND STEWS

CHAPTER 6:
GRAINS AND LEGUMES

CHAPTER 7:
VEGETARIAN AND PLANT-BASED MAINS

CHAPTER 8:
FISH AND SEAFOOD MAINS

CHAPTER 9:
POULTRY AND MEAT MAINS

CHAPTER 10:
PASTA AND PIZZA

CHAPTER 11:
DESSERTS & SWEETS

CHAPTER 12:
DRINKS AND SMOOTHIES

CHAPTER 13:
SAUCES, DRESSINGS, DIPS

CHAPTER 14:
PERSONALIZED HEALTH JOURNAL

CHAPTER 15:
THE MEDITERRANEAN DIET: ORIGINS, QUALITY, AND SUSTAINABILITY

CONCLUSION

ADDITIONAL RECIPES FOR SPECIAL OCCASIONS (10 RECIPES)

STUFFED LEG OF LAMB WITH GARLIC AND ROSEMARY

This showstopper dish uses Mediterranean herbs and slow-roasting techniques to bring out the best flavors of lamb, a central dish for holidays and family celebrations.

Includes tips on sourcing high-quality lamb and variations for different herbs.

SEAFOOD PAELLA FOR LARGE GATHERINGS

A celebratory dish from Spain, this paella features saffron-infused rice with mussels, shrimp, clams, and squid.

Provides alternative seafood options depending on availability and budget.

GRILLED SWORDFISH WITH CAPERS AND OLIVE SALSA

A perfect dish for outdoor celebrations, this recipe highlights fresh Mediterranean flavors with a zesty olive and caper salsa served on perfectly grilled swordfish.

Also includes grilling tips for other Mediterranean fish if swordfish is unavailable.

SPANAKOPITA TRIANGLES (SPINACH AND FETA PASTRIES)

These savory pastries are perfect as appetizers for parties or festive events, filled with a traditional mixture of spinach, feta, and herbs.

Variations include using other greens such as Swiss chard or adding herbs like dill and mint.

ROASTED VEGETABLE TART WITH PESTO

This colorful, eye-catching tart makes for a perfect vegetarian centerpiece at any gathering, featuring a flaky crust topped with roasted vegetables and a homemade basil pesto.

Includes options for gluten-free crust alternatives.

LAMB AND BEEF KOFTAS WITH SPICY YOGURT DIP

Perfect for sharing, these Mediterranean spiced lamb and beef koftas are served with a cooling yogurt dip. Ideal for outdoor barbecues or large gatherings.

Includes instructions for shaping and grilling the perfect koftas.

MOUSSAKA WITH EGGPLANT AND BÉCHAMEL

A classic Greek dish, Moussaka is layered with tender eggplant, flavorful minced lamb, and a creamy béchamel sauce, perfect for celebrations or family dinners.

Includes tips for making ahead and reheating, ideal for entertaining.

MOROCCAN CHICKEN TAGINE WITH APRICOTS AND ALMONDS

A festive Moroccan dish that combines sweet and savory flavors, featuring slow-cooked chicken, dried apricots, almonds, and aromatic spices.

Instructions for cooking in both traditional tagine pots and regular Dutch ovens.

BAKLAVA WITH PISTACHIOS AND HONEY

This classic Mediterranean dessert is a sweet, rich treat made with layers of filo dough, crushed pistachios, and drizzled honey, ideal for celebrations.

Offers tips on working with filo dough and variations with walnuts or almonds.

FENNEL AND ORANGE SALAD WITH POMEGRANATE SEEDS

A refreshing and vibrant salad perfect for complementing the heavier dishes during celebrations. The crunch of fennel with the sweetness of orange and pomegranate creates a delightful balance.

Suggestions on how to plate and serve this elegant salad at gatherings.

INTRODUCTION

WELCOME TO THE MEDITERRANEAN WAY OF LIFE

Welcome to the Mediterranean diet cookbook, a gateway to a healthier, more vibrant lifestyle rooted in the culinary traditions of the Mediterranean region. This book is more than just a collection of recipes; it's an invitation to experience the essence of the Mediterranean way of life—one that celebrates the simplicity of fresh, whole foods and emphasizes the importance of balance, moderation, and enjoyment.

The Mediterranean diet is not a restrictive diet but a joyful way of eating that includes delicious, flavorful dishes made with ingredients like fruits, vegetables, whole grains, fish, olive oil, and herbs. Whether you're a seasoned cook or a beginner, this cookbook will guide you on a journey through the best that Mediterranean cuisine has to offer. From quick breakfast ideas to hearty dinners, this book will help you integrate the Mediterranean lifestyle into your daily routine.

WHY THE MEDITERRANEAN DIET?

The Mediterranean diet is widely recognized as one of the healthiest diets in the world, known for promoting heart health, longevity, and overall well-being. Numerous studies have shown that following a Mediterranean-style diet can reduce the risk of chronic diseases, including heart disease, diabetes, and certain cancers. It's also a great way to maintain a healthy weight without sacrificing flavor or satisfaction.

But what makes the Mediterranean diet stand out? It's simple: it's based on real, whole foods, and it encourages you to savor every bite. The diet includes a variety of fresh fruits and vegetables, healthy fats from olive oil, moderate amounts of fish and lean meats, whole grains, and a moderate intake of dairy products, such as cheese and yogurt.

HEALTH BENEFITS OF THE MEDITERRANEAN DIET

The Mediterranean diet is rich in nutrients that provide numerous health benefits. Here are some key reasons to adopt this lifestyle:

Heart Health: The diet emphasizes healthy fats from olive oil and fish, which are known to reduce bad cholesterol (LDL) and increase good cholesterol (HDL), improving heart health.
Weight Management: Since the Mediterranean diet focuses on whole foods and healthy fats, it supports healthy weight loss and maintenance.
Reduced Inflammation: The diet is rich in antioxidants from fruits, vegetables, and olive oil, helping reduce inflammation in the body, which can lower the risk of chronic diseases.

Longevity: Mediterranean populations, particularly in places like Greece and southern Italy, have some of the highest life expectancies in the world. Their diet is a key factor in their long, healthy lives.

MEDITERRANEAN FOOD PYRAMID EXPLAINED

The Mediterranean food pyramid is an easy guide to understand how the diet is structured:

Base of the Pyramid: Daily servings of vegetables, fruits, whole grains, legumes, and nuts.

Healthy Fats: Olive oil should be the primary source of fat in your diet, used in cooking, dressings, and sauces.

Protein: Include fish and seafood at least twice a week, while poultry, eggs, cheese, and yogurt can be enjoyed in moderation.

Limited Red Meat: Red meat is consumed sparingly in the Mediterranean diet, usually reserved for special occasions.

Wine: A small amount of red wine (typically a glass per day) is common, but entirely optional.

ESSENTIAL INGREDIENTS FOR YOUR MEDITERRANEAN PANTRY

Before you start cooking, it's helpful to stock your pantry with essential Mediterranean ingredients. Here are the staples you'll need:

Olive Oil: Use extra virgin olive oil for cooking, drizzling, and dressings.

Fresh Vegetables: Tomatoes, cucumbers, eggplants, bell peppers, and leafy greens are must-haves.

Whole Grains: Stock up on bulgur, quinoa, couscous, farro, and whole-wheat pasta.

Legumes: Chickpeas, lentils, and beans are great sources of plant-based protein.

Fish and Seafood: Salmon, sardines, tuna, and shellfish are Mediterranean diet staples.

Herbs and Spices: Oregano, basil, mint, rosemary, thyme, and garlic will bring authentic flavors to your dishes.

TIPS FOR GETTING STARTED

Transitioning to the Mediterranean diet is easy when you focus on the basics:

Start with Small Changes: Swap butter for olive oil, replace processed snacks with nuts or fresh fruit, and aim to include more vegetables in every meal.

Plan Your Meals: Meal planning helps ensure you have healthy options readily available, especially during busy weekdays.

Cook at Home: Preparing meals at home allows you to control the quality of ingredients and reduce your intake of processed foods.

HOW TO USE THIS BOOK

This book is structured to help you seamlessly integrate the Mediterranean diet into your life. You'll find a 30-day meal plan that simplifies grocery shopping and meal prep, along with a wide variety of recipes for every occasion. Whether you're looking for quick breakfasts, hearty dinners, or snacks, each chapter will guide you through easy-to-follow, delicious Mediterranean dishes.

The recipes are organized by meal type, from breakfast to desserts, so you can easily find what you need. Each recipe is accompanied by nutritional information, serving suggestions, and tips to enhance your cooking experience. Whether you're cooking for yourself or feeding a family, this book will provide endless inspiration for enjoying Mediterranean cuisine.

MEAL PLANNING MADE EASY

A big part of the Mediterranean diet's success is its simplicity in meal planning. You don't need fancy or expensive ingredients to follow this diet. In this book, you will find:

A **30-day meal plan** that covers breakfast, lunch, and dinner, making it easy to stay on track.
Weekly grocery shopping lists that save you time and ensure you have everything you need for the week ahead.
Easy prep tips that show you how to cook efficiently and with minimal stress.

GROCERY SHOPPING GUIDE: CHOOSING THE BEST INGREDIENTS

The Mediterranean diet encourages using the freshest ingredients you can find. Here's what to look for when grocery shopping:

Fruits and Vegetables: Choose organic when possible, and focus on seasonal produce for the best flavor and nutrition.
Seafood: Opt for sustainably sourced fish and shellfish.
Whole Grains: Look for whole-grain options, such as quinoa, farro, and whole-wheat pasta, in place of refined grains.
Dairy: Choose plain yogurt, feta, or goat cheese in moderation.
Herbs and Spices: Fresh herbs will elevate your dishes, but dried versions are a convenient and flavorful alternative.

THE ROLE OF OLIVE OIL, HERBS, AND SPICES IN MEDITERRANEAN CUISINE

Olive oil is the cornerstone of Mediterranean cooking, not just for its flavor but for its health benefits. Always opt for extra virgin olive oil, which is the least processed and has the highest levels of antioxidants. Herbs like oregano, basil, rosemary, and thyme, combined with spices like cumin and paprika, are key to creating flavorful Mediterranean dishes without relying on salt.

CHAPTER 1:

EXCLUSIVE 30-DAY MEAL PLAN

This 30-day meal plan will guide you through balanced breakfasts, lunches, and dinners for an entire month, offering a variety of Mediterranean dishes to keep your palate interested and your meals nutritious.

MEAL PLAN

1 week

	BREAKFAST	LUNCH	DINNER
1 DAY	Greek Yogurt with Honey and Nuts - 20	Greek Salad with Feta - 37	Grilled Salmon with Lemon and Dill - 78
2 DAY	Oatmeal with Dried Figs and Almonds - 26	Lentil Salad with Fresh Herbs - 40	Mediterranean Chicken Stew with Olives - 91
3 DAY	Spinach and Feta Omelet - 21	Tabbouleh with Parsley and Bulgur - 38	Baked Cod with Tomatoes and Olives - 79
4 DAY	Mediterranean Avocado Toast - 22	Caprese Salad with Basil - 39	Roasted Chicken with Lemon and Rosemary - 89
5 DAY	Whole-Grain Pancakes with Fruit - 24	Cucumber and Tomato Salad with Mint - 41	Grilled Vegetable Kebabs with Tzatziki - 68
6 DAY	Chickpea Flour Scramble with Veggies - 25	Quinoa Salad with Roasted Vegetables - 42	Shrimp Saganaki with Feta and Tomato - 80
7 DAY	Shakshuka (Eggs in Tomato Sauce) - 27	Warm Farro Salad with Sun-Dried Tomatoes - 45	Moroccan Lamb Stew - 56

 1 week

GROCERY SHOPPING LIST

PRODUCE:
- spinach
- tomatoes
- cucumbers
- lettuce
- parsley
- mint
- basil
- lemon
- olives
- sun-dried tomatoes fresh herbs

DAIRY:
- greek yogurt
- feta cheese

GRAINS:
- whole-grain oats
- bulgur
- farro
- quinoa

PROTEINS:
- chicken breast
- cod
- salmon
- shrimp
- lamb
- chickpeas

OTHER:
- olive oil
- nuts (almonds, walnuts)
- honey

Scan the code for the grocery list with precise ingredient measurements:

MEAL PLAN

2 week

	BREAKFAST	LUNCH	DINNER
8 DAY	Greek Yogurt with Honey and Walnuts - 20	Tomato and Olive Flatbread - 23	Grilled Sardines with Garlic and Parsley - 82
9 DAY	Spinach and Feta Omelet - 21	Lentil Soup with Lemon - 48	Baked Trout with Herbs and Almonds - 86
10 DAY	Oatmeal with Dried Figs and Almonds - 26	Roasted Vegetables with Thyme - 44	Tuna Salad with Capers and Olives - 81
11 DAY	Mediterranean Avocado Toast - 22	Greek Tzatziki with Pita Bread - 33	Roasted Cauliflower with Lemon and Capers - 74
12 DAY	Whole-Grain Pancakes with Fruit - 24	Caprese Salad with Basil - 39	Grilled Lamb Chops with Garlic and Thyme - 92
13 DAY	Shakshuka (Eggs in Tomato Sauce) - 27	Quinoa Salad with Herbs - 42	Eggplant Parmesan with Basil - 71
14 DAY	Chickpea Flour Scramble with Veggies - 25	Cucumber and Tomato Salad with Mint - 41	Mediterranean Fish Stew with Tomatoes and Herbs - 52

2 week ## GROCERY SHOPPING LIST

PRODUCE:
- eggplant
- tomatoes
- cucumbers
- parsley
- thyme
- basil
- mint
- garlic
- lemon

DAIRY:
- greek yogurt
- feta cheese
- ricotta

GRAINS:
- whole-grain oats
- quinoa
- bulgur

PROTEINS:
- trout
- sardines
- lamb
- tuna
- chickpeas
- lentils

OTHER:
- olive oil
- nuts (almonds)
- pita bread

Scan the code for the grocery list with precise ingredient measurements:

MEAL PLAN

3 week

	BREAKFAST	LUNCH	DINNER
15 DAY	Greek Yogurt with Honey and Nuts - 20	Greek Salad with Feta - 37	Grilled Calamari with Lemon and Garlic - 87
16 DAY	Whole-Grain Pancakes with Fresh Fruit - 24	Tabbouleh with Parsley and Bulgur - 38	Chicken Tagine with Apricots and Almonds - 93
17 DAY	Spinach and Feta Omelet - 21	Lentil Salad with Fresh Herbs and Lemon - 40	Shrimp Pasta with Lemon and Capers - 105
18 DAY	Mediterranean Avocado Toast - 22	Caprese Salad with Basil - 39	Grilled Vegetable Kebabs with Tzatziki - 68
19 DAY	Oatmeal with Dried Figs and Almonds - 26	Roasted Red Pepper Dip with Veggies - 34	Mediterranean Pizza with Olives and Feta - 103
20 DAY	Chickpea Flour Scramble with Veggies - 25	Warm Farro Salad with Olives - 45	Grilled Chicken with Lemon and Olive Oil - 89
21 DAY	Shakshuka (Eggs in Tomato Sauce) - 27	Mediterranean Couscous with Lemon - 43	Grilled Salmon with Dill and Capers - 78

 3 week

GROCERY SHOPPING LIST

PRODUCE:
- figs
- spinach
- cucumbers
- tomatoes
- bell peppers
- parsley
- mint
- garlic
- lemon
- olives

DAIRY:
- greek yogurt
- feta cheese

GRAINS:
- whole-grain oats
- bulgur
- farro
- couscous

PROTEINS:
- chicken breast
- calamari
- shrimp
- salmon
- chickpeas

OTHER:
- olive oil
- honey
- pita bread

Scan the code for the grocery list with precise ingredient measurements:

MEAL PLAN

4 week

	BREAKFAST	LUNCH	DINNER
22 DAY	*Greek Yogurt with Honey and Walnuts - 20*	*Caprese Salad with Basil - 39*	*Baked Cod with Tomatoes and Olives - 79*
23 DAY	*Spinach and Feta Omelet - 21*	*Roasted Vegetable Salad with Thyme - 44*	*Grilled Lamb Chops with Garlic and Thyme - 92*
24 DAY	*Oatmeal with Dried Figs and Almonds - 26*	*Greek Tzatziki with Pita Bread - 33*	*Mediterranean Paella with Saffron - 84*
25 DAY	*Mediterranean Avocado Toast - 22*	*Quinoa Salad with Roasted Vegetables - 42*	*Grilled Chicken Souvlaki with Tzatziki - 88*
26 DAY	*Whole-Grain Pancakes with Fresh Fruit - 24*	*Greek Salad with Feta - 37*	*Shrimp Saganaki with Feta and Tomato - 80*
27 DAY	*Shakshuka (Eggs in Tomato Sauce) - 27*	*Warm Farro Salad with Sun-Dried Tomatoes - 45*	*Chicken Stew with Olives and Lemon - 91*
28 DAY	*Chickpea Flour Scramble with Veggies - 25*	*Mediterranean Couscous with Lemon - 43*	*Grilled Sardines with Garlic and Olive Oil - 82*

4 week

GROCERY SHOPPING LIST

PRODUCE:
- figs
- spinach
- tomatoes
- bell peppers
- parsley
- mint
- garlic
- lemon
- olives
- saffron

DAIRY:
- greek yogurt
- feta cheese

GRAINS:
- whole-grain oats
- bulgur
- farro
- couscous
- quinoa

PROTEINS:
- chicken breast
- cod
- lamb
- shrimp
- sardines
- chickpeas

OTHER:
- olive oil
- nuts
- pita bread

Scan the code for the grocery list with precise ingredient measurements:

MEAL PREPARATION TIPS

Prepping for the Week: Set aside time on the weekend to prepare some of the longer-cooking items, such as grains (quinoa, bulgur, couscous) and roasted vegetables. Store them in airtight containers for easy use during the week.

Batch Cooking: Consider cooking larger portions of recipes like soups, stews, or grain dishes so that you have leftovers for lunch the next day.

Seasoning in Advance: Marinate proteins like chicken, lamb, or fish ahead of time and refrigerate for enhanced flavor and quick cooking during the week.

Use Fresh Herbs: Mediterranean cuisine thrives on the use of fresh herbs, so don't hesitate to use parsley, mint, basil, and thyme generously in your meals.

CHAPTER 2:

BREAKFAST DELIGHTS

2 servings
10 minutes

Savory Greek Yogurt Bowl with Cucumber and Herbs

Nutritional Information (per serving):

Calories:	180 kcal
Protein:	14 g
Fats:	9 g
Carbs:	8 g

NB Low-Calorie, Refreshing Breakfast Option, Perfect for Summer Mornings

Ingredients:

- 2 cups plain Greek yogurt
- 1 small cucumber (grated or finely diced)
- 2 tbsp fresh dill (chopped)
- 1 tbsp fresh mint (chopped)
- 1 tbsp olive oil
- 1 clove garlic (minced)
- salt and pepper to taste
- 2 tbsp pumpkin seeds (optional, for garnish)

Instructions:

1 *In a bowl,* mix the Greek yogurt, cucumber, dill, mint, olive oil, and minced garlic.

2 *Season with salt and pepper,* adjusting to taste.

3 *Divide the mixture* into two bowls and drizzle with a little extra olive oil.

4 *Top with pumpkin seeds* for a crunch, if desired.

 All ingredients are readily available at Walmart, Target, and Whole Foods in the dairy, produce, and condiment aisles.

The whole process with color photos

Sweet Potato Breakfast Hash with Poached Eggs

servings 2

minutes 20

Nutritional Information (per serving):

Calories:	320 kcal
Protein:	12 g
Fats:	14 g
Carbs:	40 g

NB High-Protein, Family-Friendly, Ideal for Weekend Breakfast

Ingredients:

- 2 medium sweet potatoes (peeled and diced)
- 1 tbsp olive oil
- 1 small onion (diced)
- 1 bell pepper (diced)
- 2 cloves garlic (minced)
- 1 tsp paprika
- salt and pepper to taste
- 2 large eggs (poached)
- fresh parsley (for garnish)

Instructions:

1 *Heat olive oil* in a large skillet over medium heat.

2 *Add the diced sweet potatoes* and cook for 10 minutes, stirring occasionally, until they start to soften.

3 *Add the onion, bell pepper, and garlic,* cooking for another 5 minutes until the vegetables are tender.

4 *Season with paprika, salt, and pepper.*

5 *Poach the eggs* separately by bringing water to a simmer in a small pot and carefully cracking the eggs into the water, cooking for about 3-4 minutes until the whites are set.

6 *Top the sweet potato hash with the poached eggs and garnish with fresh parsley.*

You can find all ingredients at Publix, Aldi, and Costco in the produce and dairy sections

The whole process with color photos

Greek Yogurt with Honey and Nuts

Nutritional Information (per serving):

2 servings
5 minutes

Calories: 250 kcal
Protein: 15 g
Fats: 12 g
Carbs: 20 g

Ingredients:

- 2 cups Greek yogurt (plain, unsweetened)
- 2 tbsp honey
- ¼ cup mixed nuts (walnuts, almonds, or pistachios)
- 1 tsp chia seeds (optional)

NB Family-Friendly, Low-Calorie Option, Perfect for Quick Breakfasts

Instructions:

1. *Spoon the yogurt* into two serving bowls.
2. *Drizzle the honey* over the yogurt in each bowl.
3. *Sprinkle the nuts* and chia seeds on top.
4. *Serve immediately* or refrigerate for later.

All ingredients can be found at supermarkets like Walmart, Whole Foods, and Publix in the dairy and baking aisles.

The whole process with color photos

Spinach and Feta Omelet

Nutritional Information (per serving):

Calories:	300 kcal
Protein:	20 g
Fats:	22 g
Carbs:	3 g

Ingredients:

- 4 large eggs
- 1 cup fresh spinach (chopped)
- 1/4 cup feta cheese (crumbled)
- 1 tbsp olive oil
- salt and pepper to taste

servings **2**

minutes **10**

 Family-Friendly, Low-Carb Option, Great for Busy Mornings

Instructions:

1 *Whisk the eggs* in a bowl and season with salt and pepper.
2 *Heat the olive oil* in a non-stick skillet over medium heat.
3 *Sauté the spinach* until wilted, about 2 minutes.
4 *Pour the eggs* over the spinach and cook until set, about 5 minutes.
5 *Sprinkle the feta* cheese over one half of the omelet.
6 *Fold the omelet* in half and serve immediately.

All ingredients are available at Costco, Target, and Whole Foods in the produce and dairy sections.

The whole process with color photos

Mediterranean Avocado Toast

**Nutritional Information
(per serving):**

🌙 **2** servings

🕐 **10** minutes

Calories:	350 kcal
Protein:	8 g
Fats:	30 g
Carbs:	28 g

NB Perfect for Date Night Brunches, Easy to Share with Friends

Ingredients:
- 2 slices of whole-grain bread (toasted)
- 1 ripe avocado
- 2 tbsp olive oil
- 1 tbsp lemon juice
- $1/4$ cup cherry tomatoes (halved)
- 2 tbsp feta cheese (crumbled)
- salt and pepper to taste

Instructions:
1. *Mash the avocado* in a bowl with olive oil, lemon juice, salt, and pepper.
2. *Spread the avocado mixture* evenly on the toasted bread slices.
3. *Top with cherry tomatoes* and sprinkle with feta cheese.
4. *Serve immediately*.

🛒 *You can find all ingredients at Publix, Aldi, and Harris Teeter in the produce and bakery sections.*

The whole process with color photos

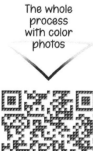

Tomato and Olive Breakfast Flatbread

Nutritional Information (per serving):

Calories:	320 kcal
Protein:	10 g
Fats:	18 g
Carbs:	30 g

Ingredients:

- 1 flatbread or pita bread
- 2 tbsp olive oil
- 1 cup cherry tomatoes (halved)
- ¼ cup Kalamata olives (pitted and sliced)
- ¼ cup feta cheese (crumbled)
- 1 tsp oregano
- salt and pepper to taste

servings 2

minutes 15

NB Family-Friendly, Ideal for Mediterranean-Themed Brunches

Instructions:

1 *Preheat the oven* to 375°F (190°C).

2 *Brush the flatbread* with olive oil and season with salt and pepper.

3 *Top with cherry tomatoes, olives, and feta cheese.*

4 *Bake in the oven* for 8-10 minutes, until the edges are crispy.

5 *Sprinkle with oregano* before serving.

All ingredients can be found at Target, Walmart, and Whole Foods in the bakery, deli, and produce sections.

The whole process with color photos

Whole-Grain Pancakes with Fresh Fruit

**Nutritional Information
(per serving):**

2 servings

15 minutes

Calories:	280 kcal
Protein:	8 g
Fats:	12 g
Carbs:	34 g

Ingredients:

- 1 cup whole-grain pancake mix
- 1 egg
- ½ cup almond milk (or any milk)
- 1 tbsp olive oil
- ½ cup mixed fresh fruit (e.g., berries, bananas, or apples)

 NB Perfect for Weekend Brunches, Family-Friendly

Instructions:

1. *Mix the* **pancake batter** by combining the pancake mix, egg, almond milk, and olive oil in a bowl.
2. **Heat a skillet** over medium heat and lightly grease it with olive oil.
3. **Pour the batter** into the skillet, forming small pancakes.
4. **Cook each side** for about 2-3 minutes, until golden brown

All ingredients can be found at Aldi, Food Lion, and Costco in the baking, dairy, and produce sections.

The whole process with color photos

Chickpea Flour Scramble with Vegetables

Nutritional Information (per serving):

Calories:	220 kcal
Protein:	10 g
Fats:	10 g
Carbs:	25 g

Ingredients:

- 1 cup chickpea flour
- ½ cup water
- 1 tbsp olive oil
- ½ cup spinach (chopped)
- ½ cup bell pepper (diced)
- salt and pepper to taste

NB Plant-Based, Gluten-Free, High-Protein Option

servings 2

minutes 10

Instructions:

1 *Mix the chickpea flour* and water in a bowl until smooth.
2 *Heat olive oil* in a skillet over medium heat.
3 *Add the vegetables* to the skillet and sauté for 3 minutes.
4 *Pour the chickpea batter* over the vegetables and cook like a scramble for 5 minutes.
5 *Season with salt and pepper,* and serve.

All ingredients can be found at Whole Foods, Publix, and Walmart in the gluten-free and produce sections

The whole process with color photos

Oatmeal with Dried Figs and Almonds

**Nutritional Information
(per serving):**

◯ **2** servings

🕐 **10** minutes

Calories:	300 kcal
Protein:	8 g
Fats:	10 g
Carbs:	40 g

Ingredients:

- 1 cup rolled oats
- 2 cups water or almond milk
- ¹/₄ cup dried figs (chopped)
- 2 tbsp almonds (chopped)
- 1 tsp cinnamon
- honey to taste

NB High-Fiber, Perfect for Cold Mornings

Instructions:

1 *Bring the water or almond milk* to a boil in a saucepan.

2 *Add the oats* and reduce to a simmer for 5 minutes, stirring occasionally.

3 *Stir in the dried figs, almonds, and cinnamon,* and cook for an additional 2 minutes.

4 *Serve topped with a drizzle of honey.*

🛒 *All ingredients can be found at Costco, Target, and Whole Foods in the breakfast and dried fruit sections.*

The whole process with color photos

Shakshuka (Eggs in Tomato Sauce)

Nutritional Information (per serving):

Calories:	250 kcal
Protein:	10 g
Fats:	14 g
Carbs:	20 g

NB Family-Friendly, Perfect for Weekend Brunches

servings 2

minutes 15

Ingredients:

- 2 tbsp olive oil
- 1 small onion (diced)
- 1 bell pepper (diced)
- 1 can (14 oz) diced tomatoes
- 2 large eggs
- 1 tsp cumin
- 1 tsp paprika
- salt and pepper to taste
- fresh parsley (for garnish)

Instructions:

1. *Heat olive oil* in a large skillet over medium heat.
2. *Sauté the onion and bell pepper* for 5 minutes, until soft.
3. *Stir in the diced tomatoes,* cumin, paprika, salt, and pepper, and simmer for 10 minutes.
4. *Make two small wells* in the tomato mixture and crack the eggs into each well.
5. *Cover the skillet* and cook for 5-6 minutes, until the eggs are set to your liking.
6. *Garnish with fresh parsley* and serve.

All ingredients can be found at Walmart, Harris Teeter, and Whole Foods in the produce and canned goods sections.

The whole process with color photos

CHAPTER 3:

APPETIZERS AND SNACKS

⏺ **2** servings
🕐 **10** minutes

Classic Hummus

Nutritional Information (per serving):

Calories:	220 kcal
Protein:	8 g
Fats:	14 g
Carbs:	18 g

Ingredients:

- 1 can (15 oz) chickpeas, drained
- 2 tbsp tahini
- 1 clove garlic
- 2 tbsp lemon juice
- 2 tbsp olive oil
- salt to taste
- water as needed (for texture)

NB Vegan, Family-Friendly, Easy to Make

Instructions:

1 *In a food processor,* combine chickpeas, tahini, garlic, lemon juice, and olive oil.

2 *Blend until smooth,* adding water as needed to achieve the desired consistency.

3 *Season with salt* to taste and drizzle with olive oil before serving.

🛒 *Available at Walmart, Target, Whole Foods in the canned goods and international food sections.*

The whole process with color photos

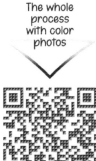

Baba Ganoush (Roasted Eggplant Dip)

Nutritional Information (per serving):

Calories:	150 kcal
Protein:	3 g
Fats:	12 g
Carbs:	10 g

 Vegan, Gluten-Free

Ingredients:
- 1 large eggplant
- 2 tbsp tahini
- 1 tbsp lemon juice
- 2 cloves garlic (minced)
- 1 tbsp olive oil
- salt and pepper to taste

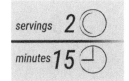

servings 2
minutes 15

Instructions:
1 **Roast the eggplant** on a gas burner or in an oven at 400°F for 25-30 minutes until charred and soft.
2 **Peel the skin** off the roasted eggplant and mash the flesh in a bowl.
3 **Add tahini, lemon juice, garlic,** olive oil, salt, and pepper. Mix until smooth.

Ingredients are readily available at Publix, Whole Foods, and Costco.

The whole process with color photos

Stuffed Grape Leaves (Dolmas)

**Nutritional Information
(per serving):**

🌙 **10** dolmas

🕐 **45** minutes

Calories:	60 kcal
Protein:	1 g
Fats:	2 g
Carbs:	9 g

NB Vegan, Great for Sharing

Ingredients:

- 20 grape leaves (from a jar)
- 1 cup cooked rice
- 2 tbsp pine nuts
- 2 tbsp raisins
- 1 tbsp fresh parsley (chopped)
- 2 tbsp lemon juice
- salt and pepper to taste

Instructions:

1 *Lay out grape leaves* and fill each with a small spoonful of rice, pine nuts, raisins, and parsley.

2 *Roll the leaves tightly,* folding in the sides, and place them in a pot.

3 *Cover with water* and add lemon juice. Simmer for 30 minutes.

🛒 *Grape leaves and other ingredients can be found at Whole Foods, Aldi, and Publix.*

The whole process with color photos

Mediterranean Veggie Platters with Dips

Nutritional Information (per serving):

Calories:	180 kcal
Protein:	5 g
Fats:	10 g
Carbs:	18 g

Ingredients:

- 1 cucumber (sliced)
- 1 bell pepper (sliced)
- 1 small carrot (sliced)
- 1 small zucchini (sliced)
- 1 cup hummus (recipe above)
- 1 cup baba ganoush (recipe above)
- 1 cup tzatziki (recipe below)

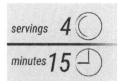

servings 4

minutes 15

 Perfect for Parties, Healthy Snack

Instructions:

1 **Arrange vegetables** on a platter.

2 **Serve with dips** like hummus, baba ganoush, and tzatziki for a colorful, shareable snack.

All ingredients can be found at Costco, Walmart, Whole Foods.

The whole process with color photos

Marinated Olives and Feta Cheese

Nutritional Information (per serving):

4 servings

10 minutes

Calories: 150 kcal
Protein: 6 g
Fats: 14 g
Carbs: 3 g

Ingredients:

- 1 cup mixed olives
- ¹/₂ cup feta cheese (cubed)
- 2 tbsp olive oil
- 1 tsp fresh thyme
- 1 tsp fresh oregano

NB Perfect for Sharing, Easy to Make

Instructions:

1 *In a bowl,* combine olives, feta, olive oil, thyme, and oregano.

2 *Let marinate* for 1 hour in the refrigerator before serving.

Available at Harris Teeter, Costco, and Whole Foods.

The whole process with color photos

Greek Tzatziki with Pita Bread

**Nutritional Information
(per serving):**

Calories:	220 kcal
Protein:	8 g
Fats:	9 g
Carbs:	26 g

Ingredients:

- 1 cup Greek yogurt
- 1 cucumber (grated)
- 2 tbsp fresh dill (chopped)
- 1 tbsp lemon juice
- 1 clove garlic (minced)
- 1 salt to taste
- 2 pita breads (cut into triangles)

NB Refreshing Dip, Family-Friendly

servings 2

minutes 10

Instructions:

1 *Mix yogurt,* cucumber, dill, lemon juice, and garlic in a bowl.

2 *Season with salt* and serve with pita bread.

Find all ingredients at Walmart, Publix, and Whole Foods.

The whole process with color photos

Roasted Red Pepper Dip (Muhammara)

Nutritional Information (per serving):

2 servings

15 minutes

Calories: 200 kcal
Protein: 3 g
Fats: 17 g
Carbs: 9 g

NB Vegan, Gluten-Free, Smoky Flavor

Ingredients:

- 2 roasted red peppers (from a jar or fresh)
- ¼ cup walnuts
- 1 tbsp pomegranate molasses
- 2 tbsp olive oil
- 1 clove garlic (minced)
- salt to taste

Instructions:

1 **In a food processor,** blend roasted peppers, walnuts, molasses, olive oil, and garlic until smooth.

2 **Season with salt** and serve chilled.

Ingredients available at Whole Foods, Aldi, and Publix.

The whole process with color photos

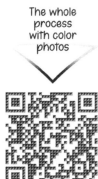

Spiced Chickpeas for Snacking

Nutritional Information (per serving):

Calories:	180 kcal
Protein:	8 g
Fats:	6 g
Carbs:	20 g

Ingredients:

- 1 can chickpeas (drained and rinsed)
- 1 tbsp olive oil
- 1 tsp paprika
- 1 tsp cumin
- salt and pepper to taste

servings 2

minutes 5

NB High-Protein Snack, Easy to Pack for Work or School

Instructions:

1 **Toss chickpeas** with olive oil, paprika, cumin, salt, and pepper.

2 **Bake at 400°F** for 20-25 minutes until crispy.

All ingredients can be found at Walmart, Target, and Publix.

The whole process with color photos

Tapenade with Grilled Bread

2 servings

10 minutes

Nutritional Information (per serving):

Calories:	180 kcal
Protein:	2 g
Fats:	16 g
Carbs:	6 g

Ingredients:
- ½ cup black olives (pitted)
- 1 tbsp capers
- 1 clove garlic (minced)
- 1 tbsp olive oil
- 1 tsp lemon juice
- grilled bread slices for serving

NB Perfect Appetizer for Date Night

Instructions:

1 *In a food processor,* pulse olives, capers, garlic, olive oil, and lemon juice until chunky.

2 *Serve with grilled bread.*

Find all ingredients at Aldi, Harris Teeter, and Costco.

The whole process with color photos

CHAPTER 4:

SALADS AND SIDES

Greek Salad with Feta and Olive Oil

servings 2

minutes 10

Nutritional Information (per serving):

Calories:	250 kcal
Protein:	7 g
Fats:	22 g
Carbs:	10 g

NB Classic Mediterranean Salad, Gluten-Free

Ingredients:

- 1 cucumber (sliced)
- 2 tomatoes (chopped)
- 1 small red onion (sliced)
- ½ cup feta cheese (crumbled)
- ¼ cup olives
- 2 tbsp olive oil
- salt and pepper to taste

Instructions:

1 **In a large bowl,** mix cucumber, tomatoes, onion, and olives.
2 **Top with feta,** drizzle with olive oil, and season with salt and pepper.

Find ingredients at Whole Foods, Walmart, and Publix.

The whole process with color photos

Tabbouleh (Parsley and Bulgur Salad)

Nutritional Information (per serving):

◯ **2** servings

🕒 **15** minutes

Calories: 190 kcal
Protein: 4 g
Fats: 8 g
Carbs: 25 g

NB Vegan, Rich in Fiber

Ingredients:

- ¹/₂ cup bulgur wheat
- 1 bunch fresh parsley (chopped)
- ¹/₄ cup fresh mint (chopped)
- 2 tomatoes (chopped)
- 1 small cucumber (chopped)
- 2 tbsp lemon juice
- 2 tbsp olive oil
- salt and pepper to taste

Instructions:

1 *Cook the bulgur wheat* according to the package instructions and let it cool.

2 *In a large bowl,* combine parsley, mint, tomatoes, cucumber, and cooled bulgur.

3 *Drizzle with olive oil and lemon juice,* then season with salt and pepper. Mix well.

 *All ingredients are available at Whole Foods, Publix, Aldi, and Walmart.*

The whole process with color photos

Caprese Salad with Basil and Olive Oil

**Nutritional Information
(per serving):**

Calories:	280 kcal
Protein:	12 g
Fats:	20 g
Carbs:	10 g

 Gluten-Free, Fresh and Flavorful

Ingredients:
- 2 ripe tomatoes (sliced)
- 4 oz fresh mozzarella (sliced)
- 10 fresh basil leaves
- 2 tbsp olive oil
- 1 tbsp balsamic vinegar
- salt and pepper to taste

servings 2

minutes 10

Instructions:
1 *Arrange tomato and mozzarella slices* alternately on a plate.
2 *Place basil leaves* between the slices.
3 *Drizzle with olive oil and balsamic vinegar,* then season with salt and pepper.

Ingredients can be found at Costco, Whole Foods, and Publix.

The whole process with color photos

Lentil Salad with Fresh Herbs and Lemon

**Nutritional Information
(per serving):**

2 servings

20 minutes

Calories:	240 kcal
Protein:	12 g
Fats:	9 g
Carbs:	30 g

 NB High in Protein, Vegan

Ingredients:
- 1 cup cooked green lentils
- 1/4 cup chopped parsley
- 2 tbsp fresh mint (chopped)
- 1 small red onion (chopped)
- 2 tbsp lemon juice
- 2 tbsp olive oil
- salt and pepper to taste

Instructions:

1 *In a bowl,* combine cooked lentils, parsley, mint, and onion.

2 *Drizzle with lemon juice and olive oil,* then season with salt and pepper. Toss well.

All ingredients are available at Walmart, Whole Foods, Publix, and Harris Teeter.

The whole
process
with color
photos

Cucumber and Tomato Salad with Mint

**Nutritional Information
(per serving):**

Ingredients:

Calories:	120 kcal
Protein:	2 g
Fats:	9 g
Carbs:	9 g

—1   cucumber (sliced)
—2   tomatoes (chopped)
—2   tbsp fresh mint (chopped)
—2   tbsp olive oil
—1   tbsp lemon juice
—   salt and pepper to taste

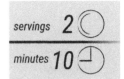

servings **2**

minutes **10**

 Refreshing, Vegan,
Gluten-Free

Instructions:

1 *Combine cucumber, tomatoes, and mint* in a bowl.

2 *Drizzle with olive oil and lemon juice,* then season with salt and pepper. Toss to mix.

All ingredients can be found at Aldi, Walmart, Target, and Costco.

The whole
process
with color
photos

Quinoa Salad with Roasted Vegetables

Nutritional Information (per serving):

2 servings

30 minutes

Calories:	250 kcal	
Protein:	6 g	
Fats:	12 g	
Carbs:	30 g	

NB Vegan, High in Fiber

Ingredients:
- ¹/₂ cup quinoa
- 1 small zucchini (chopped)
- 1 bell pepper (chopped)
- 1 small carrot (chopped)
- 2 tbsp olive oil
- 1 tsp dried oregano
- 2 tbsp lemon juice
- salt and pepper to taste

Instructions:

1. **Cook the quinoa** according to package instructions and set aside.
2. **Roast the vegetables:** Toss zucchini, bell pepper, and carrot in olive oil and roast at 400°F for 20 minutes.
3. **In a bowl,** combine the roasted vegetables with cooked quinoa.
4. **Drizzle with lemon juice** and season with oregano, salt, and pepper.

Find ingredients at Whole Foods, Publix, Harris Teeter, and Aldi.

The whole process with color photos

Mediterranean Couscous with Lemon and Herbs

Nutritional Information (per serving):

Calories:	180 kcal
Protein:	4 g
Fats:	7 g
Carbs:	26 g

Ingredients:

- ½ cup couscous
- 1 tbsp olive oil
- 2 tbsp lemon juice
- 2 tbsp fresh parsley (chopped)
- 1 tbsp fresh mint (chopped)
- salt and pepper to taste

servings 2

minutes 15

NB Easy and Quick, Family-Friendly

Instructions:

1 **Prepare couscous** according to package instructions.

2 **Stir in olive oil, lemon juice,** parsley, and mint.

3 **Season with salt and pepper** to taste. Fluff with a fork before serving.

Ingredients available at Costco, Aldi, Publix, and Walmart.

The whole process with color photos

Roasted Vegetables with Garlic and Thyme

Nutritional Information (per serving):

◷ **2** servings

⏱ **30** minutes

Calories:	200 kcal
Protein:	3 g
Fats:	14 g
Carbs:	15 g

NB Vegan, Perfect Side Dish

Ingredients:

- 1 small zucchini (chopped)
- 1 small eggplant (chopped)
- 1 red bell pepper (chopped)
- 2 cloves garlic (minced)
- 2 tbsp olive oil
- 1 tsp dried thyme
- salt and pepper to taste

Instructions:

1 *Preheat oven to 400°F.*

2 *Toss vegetables* in olive oil, garlic, thyme, salt, and pepper.

3 *Roast for 25-30 minutes,* stirring halfway through.

🛒 *Ingredients can be found at Walmart, Target, Whole Foods, and Publix.*

The whole process with color photos

Warm Farro Salad with Olives and Sun-Dried Tomatoes

Nutritional Information (per serving):

Calories:	260 kcal
Protein:	6 g
Fats:	12 g
Carbs:	30 g

 Vegan, Rich in Fiber

Ingredients:

- ¹/₂ cup farro
- ¹/₄ cup sun-dried tomatoes (chopped)
- ¹/₄ cup olives (sliced)
- 2 tbsp olive oil
- 1 tbsp lemon juice
- salt and pepper to taste

servings 2

minutes 25

Instructions:

1 **Cook farro** according to package instructions.
2 **Toss farro** with sun-dried tomatoes, olives, olive oil, and lemon juice.
3 **Season with salt and pepper** to taste.

Find ingredients at Whole Foods, Harris Teeter, and Aldi.

The whole process with color photos

Fattoush (Levantine Bread Salad)

**Nutritional Information
(per serving):**

2 *servings*

15 *minutes*

Calories:	230 kcal
Protein:	4 g
Fats:	13 g
Carbs:	26 g

NB Vegan, Gluten-Free
Option

Ingredients:

- 1 cucumber (sliced)
- 2 tomatoes (chopped)
- 1 small red onion (sliced)
- ½ pita bread (toasted and broken into pieces)
- 1 tbsp sumac
- 2 tbsp olive oil
- 1 tbsp lemon juice
- salt and pepper to taste

Instructions:

1 *Combine cucumber, tomatoes, onion,* and pita pieces in a bowl.

2 *Drizzle with olive oil, lemon juice,* and sprinkle with sumac. Season with salt and pepper, and toss to mix.

 Find ingredients at Walmart, Aldi, and Whole Foods.

The whole
process
with color
photos

Grilled Halloumi with Watermelon Salad

Nutritional Information (per serving):

Calories:	270 kcal
Protein:	9 g
Fats:	20 g
Carbs:	18 g

Ingredients:

- 4 oz halloumi cheese (sliced)
- 1/2 small watermelon (cubed)
- 2 tbsp fresh mint (chopped)
- 1 tbsp olive oil
- 1 tbsp lemon juice
- salt and pepper to taste

servings 2

minutes 15

 Sweet and Savory, Great for Summer

Instructions:

1 *Grill halloumi slices* for 2 minutes on each side until golden.

2 *In a bowl,* combine watermelon cubes, mint, olive oil, and lemon juice.

3 *Serve grilled halloumi* on top of the watermelon salad and season with salt and pepper.

Find ingredients at Whole Foods, Publix, Target, and Aldi.

The whole process with color photos

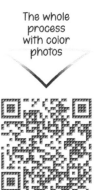

CHAPTER 5:

SOUPS AND STEWS

○ **2** servings
⏲ **10** minutes

Lentil Soup with Spinach and Lemon

Nutritional Information (per serving):

Calories:	280 kcal
Protein:	15 g
Fats:	7 g
Carbs:	40 g

NB Vegan, High in Fiber, Rich in Iron

Ingredients:

- ¹/₂ cup green or brown lentils, rinsed
- 1 small onion, chopped
- 2 cloves garlic, minced
- 4 cups vegetable broth
- 2 cups fresh spinach leaves
- 1 tbsp olive oil
- 1 tsp ground cumin
- ¹/₂ tsp ground coriander
- juice of 1 lemon
- salt and pepper to taste

Instructions:

1. **Heat olive oil** in a large pot over medium heat. Add the chopped onion and garlic and sauté for 3-4 minutes until softened.
2. **Stir in cumin and coriander** and cook for 1 minute.
3. **Add lentils and broth** to the pot, bring to a boil, then reduce the heat and simmer for 25-30 minutes until the lentils are tender.
4. **Add spinach** during the last 5 minutes of cooking, stirring until wilted.
5. **Stir in lemon juice,** season with salt and pepper to taste, and serve.

🛒 **All ingredients can be found at Whole Foods, Publix, Aldi, and Walmart.**

The whole process with color photos

Tomato Basil Soup with Olive Oil Drizzle

Nutritional Information (per serving):

Calories:	180 kcal
Protein:	4 g
Fats:	10 g
Carbs:	20 g

NB Gluten-Free, Vegan Option

Ingredients:

- 4 ripe tomatoes, chopped
- 1 small onion, chopped
- 2 cloves garlic, minced
- 2 tbsp olive oil
- 1 cup vegetable broth
- ¼ cup fresh basil leaves
- 1 tbsp balsamic vinegar
- salt and pepper to taste
- extra olive oil for drizzling

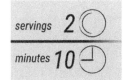

servings 2
minutes 10

Instructions:

1 *Heat olive oil* in a pot over medium heat. Sauté onion and garlic for 4-5 minutes until soft.

2 *Add chopped tomatoes* and cook for another 10 minutes until tomatoes soften.

3 *Pour in vegetable broth* and bring the soup to a simmer. Cook for 10 minutes.

4 *Add basil* and use an immersion blender to blend the soup until smooth.

5 *Season with salt, pepper, and balsamic vinegar.* Serve with a drizzle of olive oil on top.

Find ingredients at Target, Costco, and Whole Foods.

The whole process with color photos

Chickpea Soup with Paprika and Herbs

2 servings

10 minutes

Nutritional Information (per serving):

Calories: 250 kcal
Protein: 10 g
Fats: 10 g
Carbs: 30 g

 NB Vegan, High in Protein

Ingredients:

- 1 can chickpeas (15 oz), drained and rinsed
- 1 small onion, chopped
- 2 cloves garlic, minced
- 2 tbsp olive oil
- 4 cups vegetable broth
- 1 tsp smoked paprika
- 1 tsp dried thyme
- salt and pepper to taste
- 2 tbsp fresh parsley, chopped

Instructions:

1 *Heat olive oil* in a large pot and sauté onion and garlic for 3-4 minutes.
2 *Stir in smoked paprika and thyme* and cook for 1 minute.
3 *Add chickpeas and broth* and bring to a boil. Lower the heat and simmer for 20 minutes.
4 *Use a potato masher* to lightly mash some of the chickpeas to thicken the soup.
5 *Season with salt and pepper,* garnish with fresh parsley, and serve.

Available at Aldi, Walmart, Harris Teeter, and Publix.

The whole process with color photos

Avgolemono (Greek Lemon Chicken Soup)

Nutritional Information (per serving):

Calories:	230 kcal
Protein:	20 g
Fats:	8 g
Carbs:	18 g

NB Gluten-Free, Family-Friendly

Ingredients:

- 1 boneless, skinless chicken breast
- 4 cups chicken broth
- 1/4 cup orzo (or rice)
- 2 eggs
- juice of 2 lemons
- salt and pepper to taste
- fresh parsley for garnish

servings **2**

minutes **10**

Instructions:

1 *Boil the chicken breast* in the broth for about 15 minutes until fully cooked. Remove and shred the chicken.
2 *Add orzo* to the broth and cook for 8 minutes until tender.
3 *Whisk the eggs and lemon juice* together in a bowl.
4 *Slowly add a ladle of hot broth* to the egg mixture, whisking constantly, to temper the eggs.
5 *Stir the egg mixture* back into the soup and add the shredded chicken.
6 *Season with salt and pepper,* garnish with parsley, and serve.

All ingredients available at Costco, Publix, Target, and Whole Foods.

The whole process with color photos

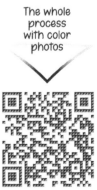

Mediterranean Fish Stew with Tomatoes and Herbs

2 servings

15 minutes

Nutritional Information (per serving):

Calories:	290 kcal
Protein:	10 g
Fats:	10 g
Carbs:	40 g

NB Rich in Omega-3, Dairy-Free

Ingredients:

- $^1/_2$ lb white fish (e.g., cod or halibut), cut into chunks
- 1 can diced tomatoes (15 oz)
- 1 small onion, chopped
- 2 cloves garlic, minced
- 2 tbsp olive oil
- $^1/_2$ cup white wine (optional)
- 2 cups fish or vegetable broth
- 1 tsp dried oregano
- 1 tsp dried basil
- salt and pepper to taste
- fresh parsley for garnish

Instructions:

1 *Heat olive oil* in a pot and sauté onion and garlic for 4-5 minutes until softened.

2 *Add diced tomatoes, white wine*, and broth, then bring to a simmer.

3 *Add the fish* and season with oregano, basil, salt, and pepper.

4 *Simmer for 10-15 minutes,* until the fish is cooked through and the flavors meld.

5 *Garnish with parsley* and serve.

All ingredients can be found at Publix, Whole Foods, and Walmart.

The whole process with color photos

Bean and Kale Soup with Garlic

Nutritional Information (per serving):

Calories:	210 kcal
Protein:	10 g
Fats:	9 g
Carbs:	24 g

NB Vegan, Packed with Nutrients

Ingredients:

- 1 can white beans (15 oz), drained and rinsed
- 2 cups kale, chopped
- 1 small onion, chopped
- 3 cloves garlic, minced
- 2 tbsp olive oil
- 4 cups vegetable broth
- salt and pepper to taste
- 1 tsp dried thyme
- 1/4 tsp red pepper flakes (optional)

servings 2
minutes 10

Instructions:

1 *Heat olive oil* in a pot and sauté onion and garlic for 3-4 minutes.
2 *Add beans, kale,* and broth, then bring to a boil.
3 *Reduce heat to simmer,* season with thyme, salt, pepper, and red pepper flakes (if using).
4 *Cook for 15 minutes* until kale is tender.
5 Serve hot with crusty bread.

Find ingredients at Aldi, Target, Costco, and Whole Foods.

The whole process with color photos

Minestrone with Seasonal Vegetables

2 servings

15 minutes

Nutritional Information (per serving):

Calories:	290 kcal
Protein:	10 g
Fats:	10 g
Carbs:	40 g

NB Vegetarian, Packed with Fiber and Vitamins

Ingredients:

- ¹/₂ cup ditalini pasta or small pasta shape
- 1 small zucchini, diced
- 1 small carrot, diced
- ¹/₂ cup spinach, chopped
- ¹/₂ cup canned cannellini beans, drained and rinsed
- ¹/₄ cup green beans, chopped
- ¹/₂ cup diced tomatoes (fresh or canned)
- 2 tbsp olive oil
- 1 small onion, chopped
- 1 clove garlic, minced
- 1 tsp dried oregano
- 3 cups vegetable broth
- salt and pepper to taste
- fresh basil for garnish

Instructions:

1. **Heat olive oil** in a large pot over medium heat. Add onion and garlic, sauté for 3-4 minutes until softened.
2. **Add carrots and zucchini,** and cook for another 5 minutes.
3. **Stir in tomatoes, green beans, and spinach,** followed by vegetable broth. Bring to a boil, then reduce heat and simmer for 15 minutes.
4. **Add pasta** and cannellini beans, simmer for another 10 minutes until the pasta is tender.
5. **Season with salt and pepper** to taste, and garnish with fresh basil before serving.

All ingredients are available at Aldi, Walmart, Publix, and Whole Foods.

The whole process with color photos

Roasted Red Pepper Soup with Yogurt

Nutritional Information (per serving):

Calories:	250 kcal
Protein:	8 g
Fats:	14 g
Carbs:	24 g

NB Creamy, Smoky, and Perfect for Cold Days

Ingredients:

- 4 large red bell peppers, roasted and peeled
- 1 small onion, chopped
- 2 tbsp olive oil
- 2 clove garlic, minced
- 1/2 tsp smoked paprika
- 2 cups vegetable broth
- 1/2 cup plain Greek yogurt
- salt and pepper to taste
- fresh parsley for garnish

servings 2

minutes 10

Instructions:

1 *Heat olive oil* in a large saucepan over medium heat. Add onion and garlic, sauté until softened, about 4-5 minutes.

2 *Add roasted peppers* and paprika. Stir and cook for 2 minutes.

3 *Pour in vegetable broth* and bring to a boil. Reduce heat and simmer for 15 minutes.

4 *Blend the soup* using an immersion blender or transfer to a blender, and process until smooth.

5 *Stir in Greek yogurt,* season with salt and pepper, and garnish with fresh parsley before serving.

Ingredients can be found at Aldi, Whole Foods, Target, and Publix.

The whole process with color photos

Moroccan-Style Lamb Stew

2 servings

15 minutes

Nutritional Information (per serving):

Calories: 450 kcal
Protein: 25 g
Fats: 25 g
Carbs: 40 g

NB Hearty, Spiced, and Comforting

Ingredients:

- ¹/₂ lb lamb shoulder, cubed
- 1 small onion, chopped
- 2 cloves garlic, minced
- 1 tbsp olive oil
- ¹/₂ tsp ground cumin
- ¹/₂ tsp ground cinnamon
- ¹/₂ tsp ground coriander
- ¹/₄ tsp cayenne pepper
- ¹/₄ cup dried apricots, chopped
- ¹/₂ can diced tomatoes
- ¹/₂ cup chickpeas, drained and rinsed
- 1 cup beef broth
- salt and pepper to taste
- fresh cilantro for garnish

Instructions:

1 *Heat olive oil* in a large pot over medium heat. Add lamb and brown on all sides, about 5-7 minutes.

2 *Add onion and garlic,* sauté for 3-4 minutes until softened.

3 *Stir in spices* (cumin, cinnamon, coriander, cayenne) and cook for 1 minute until fragrant.

4 *Add tomatoes, apricots, chickpeas,* and beef broth. Bring to a boil, then reduce heat, cover, and simmer for 45 minutes to 1 hour until lamb is tender.

5 *Season with salt and pepper,* garnish with fresh cilantro, and serve.

All ingredients can be found at Walmart, Costco, Target, and Whole Foods.

The whole process with color photos

Tuscan White Bean Soup with Rosemary

Nutritional Information (per serving):

Calories:	310 kcal
Protein:	10 g
Fats:	12 g
Carbs:	40 g

NB Rich in Fiber and Protein, Great for a Cozy Dinner

Ingredients:

- 1 cup canned cannellini beans, drained and rinsed
- 1 small onion, chopped
- 2 cloves garlic, minced
- 2 tbsp olive oil
- 1 medium carrot, diced
- 1 celery stalk, chopped
- 2 cups vegetable broth
- 1 tsp fresh rosemary, chopped (or 1/2 tsp dried rosemary)
- 1 bay leaf
- $1/4$ tsp red pepper flakes (optional)
- salt and pepper to taste
- fresh parsley for garnish
- grated Parmesan cheese for serving (optional)

servings 2

minutes 10

Instructions:

1 **Heat olive oil** in a large pot over medium heat. Add onion, garlic, carrot, and celery. Sauté for 5-7 minutes until vegetables are softened.

2 **Add cannellini beans,** rosemary, bay leaf, and red pepper flakes (if using). Stir to combine.

3 **Pour in vegetable broth** and bring the mixture to a boil. Reduce heat and let the soup simmer for 25-30 minutes, stirring occasionally.

4 **Remove the bay leaf** and use an immersion blender to blend the soup slightly for a creamier texture (optional). You can also transfer a portion of the soup to a blender and pulse.

5 **Season with salt and pepper** to taste.

6 **Serve hot,** garnished with fresh parsley and a sprinkle of grated Parmesan cheese if desired.

All ingredients are readily available at Walmart, Target, Costco, Aldi, Whole Foods, and Publix.

The whole process with color photos

CHAPTER 6:

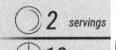

2 servings

10 minutes

GRAINS AND LEGUMES

Bulgur Pilaf with Chickpeas and Tomatoes

**Nutritional Information
(per serving):**

Calories:	320 kcal
Protein:	9 g
Fats:	10 g
Carbs:	45 g

NB Vegan, High in Fiber

Ingredients:
- ½ cup bulgur wheat
- ½ cup canned chickpeas, drained and rinsed
- ½ cup diced tomatoes (fresh or canned)
- 1 small onion, chopped
- 2 tbsp olive oil
- 1 clove garlic, minced
- ½ tsp ground cumin
- 1½ cups vegetable broth
- salt and pepper to taste
- fresh parsley for garnish

Instructions:

1 *Heat olive oil* in a saucepan over medium heat. Add onion and garlic and sauté for 3-4 minutes until softened.

2 *Stir in cumin and bulgur,* coating the grains with the oil.

3 *Add chickpeas, tomatoes,* and vegetable broth. Bring to a boil, then reduce heat, cover, and simmer for 15 minutes until the bulgur is cooked and the liquid is absorbed.

4 *Season with salt and pepper,* fluff with a fork, and garnish with fresh parsley before serving.

All ingredients available at Walmart, Aldi, Publix, and Whole Foods.

The whole process with color photos

Risotto with Mushrooms and Parmesan

Nutritional Information (per serving):

Calories:	380 kcal
Protein:	9 g
Fats:	14 g
Carbs:	52 g

NB Vegetarian, Creamy Comfort Food

Ingredients:

- ¹/₂ cup Arborio rice
- 1¹/₂ cups vegetable broth
- ¹/₂ cup mushrooms, sliced
- 1 small onion, chopped
- 2 tbsp olive oil
- 2 tbsp grated Parmesan cheese
- ¹/₄ cup white wine (optional)
- 1 clove garlic, minced
- 1 tbsp butter
- salt and pepper to taste

servings **2**

minutes **10**

Instructions:

1 *Heat olive oil* in a saucepan. Sauté onions and garlic until softened, about 3-4 minutes.

2 *Add mushrooms* and cook for another 5 minutes until they release their moisture.

3 *Stir in Arborio rice and cook* for 2 minutes to lightly toast the grains.

4 *Pour in white wine* (if using) and let it reduce by half. Begin adding vegetable broth 1/4 cup at a time, stirring continuously until absorbed.

5 *Continue adding broth,* stirring frequently, until the rice is creamy and fully cooked (about 18-20 minutes).

6 *Stir in butter and Parmesan,* season with salt and pepper, and serve.

All ingredients can be found at Target, Costco, Aldi, and Publix.

The whole process with color photos

Mediterranean Couscous with Herbs

2 servings

10 minutes

Nutritional Information (per serving):

Calories:	200 kcal
Protein:	5 g
Fats:	8g
Carbs:	28g

NB Light and Fresh, Perfect for Summer

Ingredients:

- $1/2$ cup couscous
- 1 cup vegetable broth
- 1 tbsp olive oil
- $1/4$ cup fresh parsley, chopped
- $1/4$ cup fresh mint, chopped
- juice of 1 lemon
- salt and pepper to taste

Instructions:

1 **Heat the broth** in a small saucepan until boiling. Remove from heat, stir in the couscous, cover, and let sit for 5 minutes.

2 **Fluff the couscous** with a fork and transfer to a mixing bowl.

3 **Stir in olive oil,** lemon juice, parsley, and mint. Season with salt and pepper.

4 **Serve warm or at room temperature.**

Available at Whole Foods, Aldi, Walmart, and Harris Teeter.

The whole process with color photos

Quinoa Pilaf with Nuts and Raisins

**Nutritional Information
(per serving):**

Calories:	320 kcal
Protein:	8 g
Fats:	12 g
Carbs:	42 g

NB Vegan, Gluten-Free

Ingredients:

- ¹/₂ cup quinoa, rinsed
- 1 cup vegetable broth
- ¹/₄ cup mixed nuts (e.g., almonds, pistachios), chopped
- ¹/₄ cup raisins
- 1 tbsp olive oil
- ¹/₂ tsp ground cinnamon
- salt and pepper to taste

servings **2**

minutes **10**

Instructions:

1 *Bring quinoa and vegetable broth* to a boil in a small pot. Reduce heat to low, cover, and simmer for 15 minutes until quinoa is tender.

2 *In a pan, heat olive oil* and toast the chopped nuts for 2-3 minutes.

3 *Fluff the quinoa with a fork* and mix in the nuts, raisins, cinnamon, salt, and pepper.

4 *Serve warm.*

Ingredients can be found at Costco, Publix, Target, and Whole Foods.

The whole process with color photos

Freekeh with Roasted Vegetables

Nutritional Information (per serving):

◯ **2** servings

◷ **15** minutes

Calories:	200 kcal
Protein:	10 g
Fats:	12g
Carbs:	38g

NB High in Fiber, Vegan

Ingredients:
- ¹/₂ cup freekeh
- 1 zucchini, diced
- 1 red bell pepper, diced
- 1 small eggplant, diced
- 2 tbsp olive oil
- 1 tsp dried thyme
- 1¹/₂ cups vegetable broth
- salt and pepper to taste

Instructions:

1 *Preheat the oven to 400°F.* Toss diced vegetables with olive oil, thyme, salt, and pepper. Roast for 20-25 minutes.

2 *Cook freekeh* with vegetable broth in a saucepan. Bring to a boil, reduce heat, cover, and simmer for 20 minutes until tender.

3 *Combine roasted vegetables* with cooked freekeh, season to taste, and serve warm.

🛒 *Available at Walmart, Aldi, Publix, and Whole Foods.*

The whole process with color photos

Barley Salad with Cucumber and Lemon

Nutritional Information (per serving):

Calories:	220 kcal
Protein:	5 g
Fats:	8 g
Carbs:	36 g

Ingredients:

- ¹/₂ cup pearl barley
- 1 cucumber, diced
- juice of 1 lemon
- 1 tbsp olive oil
- 1 tbsp fresh dill, chopped
- salt and pepper to taste

servings 2

minutes 10

 NB Refreshing and Light

Instructions:

1 *Cook the barley* in a pot of boiling water for 20 minutes or until tender. Drain and let cool.

2 *In a large bowl,* combine diced cucumber, lemon juice, olive oil, and dill.

3 *Add the barley,* toss to combine, and season with salt and pepper.

Available at Aldi, Target, Whole Foods, and Harris Teeter.

The whole process with color photos

Orzo with Feta and Spinach

**Nutritional Information
(per serving):**

Ingredients:

◠ **2** servings

⏱ **10** minutes

Calories:	300 kcal
Protein:	9 g
Fats:	10g
Carbs:	40g

——¹/₂ cup orzo pasta
——2 cups fresh spinach leaves
——¹/₄ cup feta cheese, crumbled
——1 tbsp olive oil
——1 clove garlic, minced
—— salt and pepper to taste

NB Vegetarian, Quick to Prepare

Instructions:

1 *Cook orzo* according to package directions, then drain.

2 *Heat olive oil* in a pan and sauté garlic for 1 minute. Add spinach and cook until wilted, about 2 minutes.

3 *Stir the cooked orzo* into the pan, mix with feta cheese, and season with salt and pepper.

 Available at Publix, Walmart, Whole Foods, and Aldi.

The whole process with color photos

Lentils with Garlic and Olive Oil

**Nutritional Information
(per serving):**

Calories:	240 kcal
Protein:	12 g
Fats:	10 g
Carbs:	28 g

Ingredients:

- ¹/₂ cup green or brown lentils
- 2 cups vegetable broth
- 3 cloves garlic, minced
- 2 tbsp olive oil
- 1 tsp dried thyme
- salt and pepper to taste

 High in Protein, Simple and Satisfying

servings 2

minutes 5

Instructions:

1 **Bring lentils and broth** to a boil in a pot. Reduce heat and simmer for 20-25 minutes until lentils are tender.

2 **Heat olive oil** in a small pan, add garlic, and sauté until fragrant.

3 **Drain lentils** and stir in garlic, olive oil, thyme, salt, and pepper.

All ingredients can be found at Target, Whole Foods, Costco, and Publix.

The whole process with color photos

Chickpea and Tomato Rice

**Nutritional Information
(per serving):**

◯ **2** servings

🕙 **10** minutes

Calories: 320 kcal
Protein: 8 g
Fats: 9g
Carbs: 50g

NB Vegan, High in Fiber

Ingredients:
- ¹/₂ cup rice (long-grain or basmati)
- ¹/₂ cup canned chickpeas, drained and rinsed
- ¹/₂ cup diced tomatoes
- 1 tbsp olive oil
- 1 small onion, chopped
- ¹/₂ tsp ground cumin
- 1¹/₂ cups vegetable broth
- salt and pepper to taste

Instructions:
1 *Heat olive oil* in a saucepan and sauté onion for 4-5 minutes.
2 *Add cumin, chickpeas, tomatoes,* and rice. Stir for 2 minutes.
3 *Pour in broth,* bring to a boil, reduce heat, cover, and simmer for 15 minutes until rice is tender.
4 *Fluff with a fork,* season with salt and pepper, and serve.

🛒 *Ingredients can be found at Aldi, Walmart, Harris Teeter, and Whole Foods.*

The whole
process
with color
photos

Farro with Mushrooms and Thyme

Nutritional Information (per serving):

Calories:	330 kcal
Protein:	12 g
Fats:	12 g
Carbs:	45 g

 Hearty and Nutritious

Ingredients:

- ¹/₂ cup farro
- 1 cup mushrooms, sliced
- 2 tbsp olive oil
- 1 small onion, chopped
- 1 clove garlic, minced
- 1 tsp dried thyme
- 1¹/₂ cups vegetable broth
- salt and pepper to taste

servings **2**

minutes **10**

Instructions:

1. *Heat olive oil* in a saucepan and sauté onions, garlic, and mushrooms for 5 minutes.
2. *Add farro* and cook for 1 minute to toast slightly.
3. *Pour in vegetable broth* and thyme, bring to a boil, reduce heat, and simmer for 20-25 minutes until farro is tender.
4. *Season with salt and pepper,* and serve warm.

Available at Publix, Whole Foods, Target, and Costco.

The whole process with color photos

CHAPTER 7:

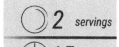

2 servings

15 minutes

VEGETARIAN AND PLANT-BASED MAINS

Grilled Vegetable Kebabs with Tzatziki

**Nutritional Information
(per serving):**

Calories:	220 kcal
Protein:	6 g
Fats:	15 g
Carbs:	18 g

NB Family-Friendly:
Great for outdoor grilling
or indoor stovetop grilling.
Can be adjusted for various
vegetables.

Ingredients:

—1 zucchini, sliced into rounds
—1 red bell pepper, cut into chunks
—1 yellow bell pepper, cut into chunks
—1 small red onion, quartered
—1 cup cherry tomatoes
—2 tbsp olive oil
—1 tsp dried oregano
— salt and pepper to taste
—4 wooden skewers,
— soaked in water for 30 minutes

For the Tzatziki:

•½ cup Greek yogurt
•1 small cucumber, grated
•1 garlic clove, minced
•1 tbsp olive oil
•1 tsp lemon juice
•salt and pepper to taste

Instructions:

1 Preheat a grill or grill pan over medium-high heat.

2 In a bowl, toss the zucchini, bell peppers, onion, and cherry tomatoes with olive oil, oregano, salt, and pepper.

3 Thread the vegetables onto the skewers. Grill the kebabs for 8–10 minutes, turning occasionally, until the vegetables are tender and slightly charred.

4 While the vegetables are grilling, prepare the tzatziki by mixing the Greek yogurt, grated cucumber, garlic, olive oil, lemon juice, salt, and pepper in a bowl.

5 Serve the kebabs with the tzatziki sauce on the side.

Available at Publix, Whole Foods, Target, and Costco.

The whole
process
with color
photos

Stuffed Bell Peppers with Quinoa and Herbs

Nutritional Information (per serving):

Calories:	250 kcal
Protein:	8 g
Fats:	10 g
Carbs:	35 g

NB Low-Calorie Option:
A light and filling dish that's perfect for lunch or dinner.

servings 2

minutes 15

Ingredients:

—2 large bell peppers (any color)
—1 cup cooked quinoa
—½ cup diced tomatoes
—1 small onion, diced
—2 garlic cloves, minced
—1 tbsp olive oil
—1 tsp dried oregano
—1 tbsp fresh parsley, chopped
—1 tbsp fresh mint, chopped
— salt and pepper to taste
—2 tbsp crumbled feta cheese (optional)

Instructions:

1. Preheat the oven to 375°F (190°C).
2. Slice the tops off the bell peppers and remove the seeds and membranes.
3. In a skillet, heat the olive oil over medium heat. Add the onion and garlic, and sauté for 5 minutes until softened.
4. Add the diced tomatoes, cooked quinoa, oregano, parsley, mint, salt, and pepper. Stir to combine and cook for 5 minutes.
5. Stuff the bell peppers with the quinoa mixture and place them in a baking dish.
6. Cover with foil and bake for 20 minutes. Remove the foil, sprinkle with feta cheese (if using), and bake for an additional 5–10 minutes until the peppers are tender.

Available at Publix, Whole Foods, Target, and Costco.

The whole process with color photos

Spanakopita (Spinach and Feta Pie)

**Nutritional Information
(per serving):**

4 servings

20 minutes

Calories: 380 kcal
Protein: 14 g
Fats: 22g
Carbs: 30g

NB Perfect for Date Night:
This savory pie makes a great
appetizer or main dish.

Ingredients:
- 1 lb fresh spinach, chopped
- 1 onion, diced
- 2 garlic cloves, minced
- 1 tbsp olive oil
- 1 cup crumbled feta cheese
- 2 eggs, beaten
- 1 tbsp fresh dill, chopped
- 8 sheets of phyllo dough, thawed
- 1/4 cup melted butter or olive oil for brushing
- salt and pepper to taste

Instructions:
1 Preheat the oven to 350°F (175°C).
2 Heat olive oil in a skillet over medium heat. Add the onion and garlic, and sauté until softened, about 5 minutes.
3 Add the spinach and cook until wilted, about 3–4 minutes. Remove from heat and let cool slightly.
4 In a large bowl, mix the cooked spinach, feta cheese, eggs, dill, salt, and pepper.
5 Lightly grease a baking dish. Layer 4 sheets of phyllo dough at the bottom, brushing each sheet with melted butter or olive oil.
6 Spread the spinach mixture over the dough, then layer the remaining phyllo sheets on top,
7 brushing each with butter or olive oil.
8 Bake for 35–40 minutes until the top is golden brown. Let cool slightly before slicing.

Available at Publix, Whole Foods, Target, and Costco.

The whole
process
with color
photos

Eggplant Parmesan with Fresh Basil

**Nutritional Information
(per serving):**

Calories:	450 kcal
Protein:	18 g
Fats:	26 g
Carbs:	40 g

NB Family-Friendly: A vegetarian classic that's perfect for family dinners.

Ingredients:

- 1 large eggplant, sliced into rounds
- 1 cup marinara sauce
- 1 cup shredded mozzarella cheese
- 1/2 cup grated Parmesan cheese
- 1 cup breadcrumbs
- 2 eggs, beaten
- 2 tbsp olive oil
- fresh basil leaves for garnish
- salt and pepper to taste

servings 2

minutes 20

Instructions:

1 Preheat the oven to 375°F (190°C).
2 Dip the eggplant slices into the beaten eggs, then coat with breadcrumbs.
3 Heat olive oil in a skillet over medium heat. Fry the eggplant slices until golden brown, about 2–3 minutes per side. Drain on paper towels.
4 In a baking dish, spread a thin layer of marinara sauce. Arrange a layer of fried eggplant slices on top, then sprinkle with mozzarella and Parmesan cheese.
Repeat the layers until all the ingredients are used, finishing with a layer of cheese.
5 Bake for 25–30 minutes until the cheese is melted and bubbly. Garnish with fresh basil leaves
6 before serving.

Available at Publix, Whole Foods, Target, and Costco.

The whole process with color photos

Falafel with Tahini Sauce

Nutritional Information (per serving):

2 servings

15 minutes

Calories: 300 kcal
Protein: 10 g
Fats: 15 g
Carbs: 35 g

NB Vegan-Friendly: A plant-based protein-rich dish perfect for any meal.

Ingredients:

- 1 can (15 oz) chickpeas, drained and rinsed
- 1 small onion, chopped
- 2 garlic cloves, minced
- 2 tbsp fresh parsley, chopped
- 1 tsp ground cumin
- 1 tsp ground coriander
- 2 tbsp flour (or chickpea flour for gluten-free)
- salt and pepper to taste
- 2 tbsp olive oil

For the Tahini Sauce:

- ¼ cup tahini
- 1 tbsp lemon juice
- 1 garlic clove, minced
- 2–3 tbsp water
- salt and pepper to taste

Instructions:

1 In a food processor, combine chickpeas, onion, garlic, parsley, cumin, coriander, flour, salt, and pepper. Pulse until a rough mixture forms.

2 Shape the mixture into small patties.

3 Heat olive oil in a skillet over medium heat. Fry the falafel patties for 3–4 minutes per side, until golden brown.

4 In a small bowl, mix tahini, lemon juice, garlic, and water until smooth. Season with salt and pepper.

5 Serve the falafel with the tahini sauce.

Available at Publix, Whole Foods, Target, and Costco.

The whole process with color photos

Vegetable Moussaka

**Nutritional Information
(per serving):**

Calories:	400 kcal
Protein:	10 g
Fats:	20 g
Carbs:	45 g

NB Perfect for Dinner Parties: A comforting and filling dish that's sure to impress.

Ingredients:

- 1 large eggplant, sliced into rounds
- 2 potatoes, sliced into rounds
- 1 zucchini, sliced into rounds
- 1 onion, diced
- 2 garlic cloves, minced
- 1 can (15 oz) crushed tomatoes
- 1 tsp ground cinnamon
- 1 tsp ground allspice
- 2 tbsp olive oil
- 1 cup béchamel sauce (made with butter, flour, and milk)
- salt and pepper to taste

servings **4**

minutes **30**

Instructions:

1 Preheat the oven to 375°F (190°C).

2 In a skillet, heat olive oil and cook the onion and garlic for 5 minutes. Add crushed tomatoes, cinnamon, allspice, salt, and pepper. Simmer for 10 minutes.

3 In another skillet, fry the eggplant, zucchini, and potato slices until golden brown. Drain on paper towels.

4 In a baking dish, layer the vegetables and tomato sauce, alternating. Top with béchamel sauce and a sprinkle of Parmesan.

5 Bake for 30–35 minutes until the top is golden brown.

Available at Publix, Whole Foods, Target, and Costco.

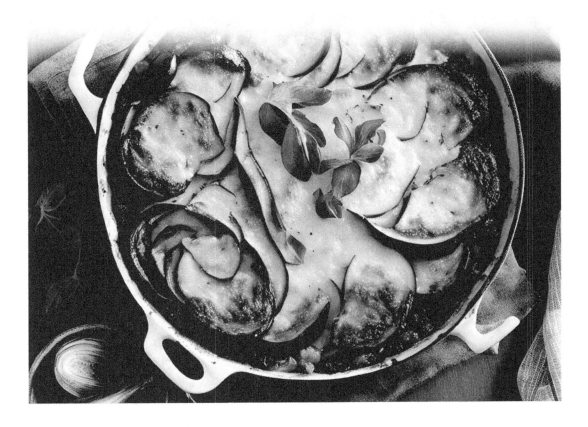

The whole process with color photos

Roasted Cauliflower with Lemon and Capers

2 servings

10 minutes

Nutritional Information (per serving):

Calories:	180 kcal
Protein:	3 g
Fats:	12g
Carbs:	15g

NB Low-Calorie Option:
A light and zesty side dish or main course for plant-based eaters.

Ingredients:

- 1 medium cauliflower, cut into florets
- 2 tbsp olive oil
- 1 tbsp capers, rinsed
- 1 lemon, zested and juiced
- 1 garlic clove, minced
- salt and pepper to taste
- fresh parsley for garnish

Instructions:

1. Preheat oven to 400°F (200°C).
2. Toss cauliflower florets with olive oil, garlic, salt, and pepper in a large bowl.
3. Spread the cauliflower on a baking sheet in a single layer.
4. Roast for 25–30 minutes until golden brown, tossing halfway through.
5. Remove from the oven and toss with lemon juice, zest, and capers.
6. Garnish with parsley and serve warm.

Available at Publix, Whole Foods, Target, and Costco.

The whole process with color photos

Ratatouille with Olive Oil and Garlic

**Nutritional Information
(per serving):**

Calories:	250 kcal
Protein:	4 g
Fats:	14 g
Carbs:	30 g

NB Family-Friendly: A great vegetable-packed dish that can be enjoyed by the whole family.

Ingredients:

- 1 eggplant, diced
- 1 zucchini, diced
- 1 red bell pepper, diced
- 1 yellow bell pepper, diced
- 1 onion, diced
- 2 garlic cloves, minced
- 2 tbsp olive oil
- 1 can (14.5 oz) diced tomatoes
- 1 tsp dried thyme
- 1 tsp dried basil
- salt and pepper to taste
- fresh basil for garnish

servings **2**

minutes **15**

Instructions:

1 Heat olive oil in a large pan over medium heat.
2 Add onion and garlic, and cook until softened, about 5 minutes.
3 Add eggplant, zucchini, and bell peppers. Cook for 10–12 minutes, stirring occasionally.
4 Add diced tomatoes, thyme, basil, salt, and pepper.
5 Simmer for 20–25 minutes until the vegetables are tender.
6 Garnish with fresh basil and serve warm.

Available at Publix, Whole Foods, Target, and Costco.

The whole process with color photos

Lentil and Veggie Shepherd's Pie

**Nutritional Information
(per serving):**

⊘ **2** *servings*

🕒 **20** *minutes*

Calories:	*350 kcal*
Protein:	*12 g*
Fats:	*10 g*
Carbs:	*55 g*

NB Perfect for Date Night:
A hearty and comforting dish
that's perfect for sharing.

Ingredients:

— 1 cup lentils, cooked
— 1 onion, diced
— 2 carrots, diced
— 1 celery stalk, diced
— 2 garlic cloves, minced
— 1 tbsp olive oil
— 1 tbsp tomato paste
— 1 cup vegetable broth
— 1 tsp thyme
— 1 tsp rosemary
— 2 medium potatoes, boiled and mashed
— 2 tbsp plant-based butter
—   salt and pepper to taste

Instructions:

1 Preheat oven to 375°F (190°C).
2 Heat olive oil in a large skillet over medium heat. Add onion, garlic, carrots, and celery. Cook until softened, about 7 minutes.
3 Stir in tomato paste, cooked lentils, vegetable broth, thyme, rosemary, salt, and pepper. Let simmer for 10 minutes.
4 Spread the lentil mixture evenly in a baking dish.
5 In a separate bowl, mix mashed potatoes with butter, and spread over the lentil mixture.
6 Bake for 20–25 minutes until the top is golden brown.

🛒 *Available at Publix, Whole Foods, Target, and Costco.*

The whole
process
with color
photos

Chickpea and Spinach Stew with Paprika

Nutritional Information (per serving):

Calories:	290 kcal
Protein:	9 g
Fats:	14 g
Carbs:	30 g

NB Low-Calorie Option: A nutrient-dense and flavorful dish that's filling yet light.

Ingredients:

- 1 can (15 oz) chickpeas, drained and rinsed
- 2 cups fresh spinach
- 1 onion, diced
- 2 garlic cloves, minced
- 2 tbsp olive oil
- 1 tsp smoked paprika
- 1 tsp ground cumin
- 1 cup vegetable broth
- 1 salt and pepper to taste

servings 2

minutes 10

Instructions:

1 Heat olive oil in a large pan over medium heat. Add onion and garlic, and cook for 5 minutes until softened.

2 Stir in smoked paprika and cumin, and cook for 1 minute.

3 Add chickpeas and vegetable broth. Simmer for 10 minutes.

4 Stir in fresh spinach and cook until wilted, about 3 minutes.

5 Season with salt and pepper to taste. Serve warm.

Available at Publix, Whole Foods, Target, and Costco.

The whole process with color photos

CHAPTER 8:

2 *servings*

10 *minutes*

FISH AND SEAFOOD MAINS

Grilled Salmon with Lemon and Dill

Nutritional Information (per serving):

Calories:	350 kcal
Protein:	35 g
Fats:	20 g
Carbs:	2 g

Ingredients:

- 2 salmon fillets (6 oz each)
- 1 tbsp olive oil
- juice of 1 lemon
- 2 tbsp fresh dill, chopped
- salt and pepper to taste
- lemon wedges for serving

 NB Perfect for Date Night: Simple yet elegant, this dish is perfect for a romantic dinner.

Instructions:

1 Preheat your grill or grill pan over medium-high heat.
2 Rub the salmon fillets with olive oil and season with salt, pepper, and half of the dill.
3 Grill the salmon for 5–6 minutes on each side until cooked through and slightly charred.
4 Drizzle with lemon juice and sprinkle the remaining dill before serving.
5 Serve with lemon wedges on the side.

Available at Publix, Whole Foods, Target, and Costco.

The whole process with color photos

Baked Cod with Tomatoes and Olives

Nutritional Information (per serving):

Calories:	250 kcal
Protein:	28 g
Fats:	10 g
Carbs:	12 g

Ingredients:
- 2 2 cod fillets (6 oz each)
- 1 1 can (15 oz) diced tomatoes
- ½ ½ cup Kalamata olives, pitted
- 1 1 tbsp capers
- 1 1 garlic clove, minced
- 1 1 tbsp olive oil
- 1 1 tsp dried oregano
-    salt and pepper to taste

servings 2

minutes 10

NB Family-Friendly: A flavorful and light dish that's perfect for a family meal.

Instructions:
1. Preheat the oven to 375°F (190°C).
2. In a baking dish, combine the diced tomatoes, olives, capers, garlic, olive oil, oregano, salt, and pepper.
3. Place the cod fillets on top of the tomato mixture.
4. Bake for 20–25 minutes until the fish is cooked through and flakes easily with a fork.
5. Serve the cod with the tomato and olive sauce spooned over the top.

Available at Publix, Whole Foods, Target, and Costco.

The whole process with color photos

Shrimp Saganaki (Shrimp in Tomato and Feta Sauce)

2 servings

20 minutes

Nutritional Information (per serving):

Calories:	350 kcal
Protein:	35 g
Fats:	18 g
Carbs:	12 g

NB Great for Sharing: Ideal for a cozy dinner with friends or family.

Ingredients:

—1   lb shrimp, peeled and deveined
—1   can (15 oz) crushed tomatoes
—1   small onion, diced
—2   garlic cloves, minced
—1   tbsp olive oil
—1/2 cup crumbled feta cheese
—1   tbsp fresh parsley, chopped
—   salt and pepper to taste

Instructions:

1 Heat olive oil in a skillet over medium heat. Add the onion and garlic and sauté for 5 minutes until softened.

2 Add the crushed tomatoes and bring to a simmer. Cook for 10 minutes, allowing the sauce to thicken.

3 Stir in the shrimp and cook for 3–4 minutes until the shrimp turn pink.

4 Remove from heat and stir in the crumbled feta and parsley.

5 Serve hot with crusty bread or over rice.

Available at Publix, Whole Foods, Target, and Costco.

The whole process with color photos

Tuna Salad with Capers and Olives

**Nutritional Information
(per serving):**

Calories:	250 kcal
Protein:	20 g
Fats:	15 g
Carbs:	5 g

NB Quick and Healthy:
Perfect for a light lunch or as
a side dish.

Ingredients:

- 1 can (5 oz) tuna in olive oil, drained
- ¼ cup Kalamata olives, sliced
- 1 tbsp capers
- 2 tbsp red onion, finely chopped
- 1 tbsp fresh parsley, chopped
- juice of 1 lemon
- 1 tbsp olive oil
- salt and pepper to taste

servings **2**

minutes **10**

Instructions:

1 In a bowl, combine the tuna, olives, capers, red onion, and parsley.
2 Drizzle with olive oil and lemon juice, then season with salt and pepper.
3 Toss gently to combine and serve.

Available at Publix, Whole Foods, Target, and Costco.

The whole
process
with color
photos

Grilled Sardines with Garlic and Parsley

Nutritional Information (per serving):

○ **2** servings

🕐 **10** minutes

Calories:	300 kcal
Protein:	30 g
Fats:	18 g
Carbs:	2 g

Ingredients:

- 6 whole sardines, cleaned
- 2 tbsp olive oil
- 2 garlic cloves, minced
- 1 tbsp fresh parsley, chopped
- juice of 1 lemon
- salt and pepper to taste

NB Ideal for Outdoor Grilling: Fresh and simple Mediterranean flavors, perfect for summertime.

Instructions:

1 Preheat the grill to medium-high heat.

2 Rub the sardines with olive oil, garlic, salt, and pepper.

3 Grill the sardines for 3–4 minutes on each side until the skin is crispy and the fish is cooked through.

4 Drizzle with lemon juice and sprinkle with parsley before serving.

 Available at Publix, Whole Foods, Target, and Costco.

The whole process with color photos

Mediterranean Fish Tacos

Nutritional Information (per serving):

Calories:	400 kcal
Protein:	30 g
Fats:	20 g
Carbs:	35 g

Ingredients:

- 2 white fish fillets (such as tilapia or cod)
- 1 tbsp olive oil
- 1 tsp paprika
- 1 tsp cumin
- salt and pepper to taste
- 4 small tortillas
- ½ cup shredded cabbage
- ¼ cup diced tomatoes
- ¼ cup crumbled feta cheese
- 2 tbsp tzatziki sauce

NB Perfect for a Quick Dinner: These tacos bring Mediterranean flavors to a classic dish.

servings **2**

minutes **15**

Instructions:

1. In a skillet, heat olive oil over medium heat. Season the fish fillets with paprika, cumin, salt, and pepper.
2. Cook the fish for 3–4 minutes on each side until cooked through.
3. Flake the fish and divide it between the tortillas.
4. Top with shredded cabbage, diced tomatoes, crumbled feta, and a drizzle of tzatziki sauce.

Available at Publix, Whole Foods, Target, and Costco.

The whole process with color photos

Seafood Paella with Saffron

Nutritional Information (per serving):

4 servings

20 minutes

Calories: 500 kcal
Protein: 35 g
Fats: 10 g
Carbs: 65 g

NB Perfect for Gatherings: A colorful and flavorful dish that's great for entertaining.

Ingredients:

- 1 cup Arborio rice
- 1 tbsp olive oil
- 1 small onion, diced
- 2 garlic cloves, minced
- 1/2 tsp saffron threads
- 1 cup diced tomatoes
- 2 cups fish stock
- 1/2 lb shrimp, peeled and deveined
- 1/2 lb mussels, cleaned
- 1/2 lb squid, sliced into rings
- 1/2 cup peas
- fresh parsley for garnish
- lemon wedges for serving

Instructions:

1. Heat olive oil in a large skillet or paella pan over medium heat. Add the onion and garlic and sauté for 5 minutes.
2. Stir in the rice and saffron, cooking for 1–2 minutes until the rice is coated in oil.
3. Add the diced tomatoes and fish stock. Bring to a simmer and cook for 15 minutes, stirring occasionally.
4. Add the shrimp, mussels, squid, and peas. Cover and cook for 10–15 minutes until the seafood is cooked and the rice is tender.
5. Garnish with fresh parsley and serve with lemon wedges.

Available at Publix, Whole Foods, Target, and Costco.

The whole process with color photos

Octopus Salad with Lemon and Olive Oil

Nutritional Information (per serving):

Calories:	250 kcal
Protein:	30 g
Fats:	12 g
Carbs:	5 g

Ingredients:

- 1 lb octopus, cleaned
- 1 tbsp olive oil
- juice of 1 lemon
- 2 garlic cloves, minced
- 1 tbsp fresh parsley, chopped
- salt and pepper to taste

servings 2

minutes 10

NB Light and Refreshing:
A Mediterranean classic,
perfect for summer meals.

Instructions:

1. In a large pot of boiling water, cook the octopus for 30–40 minutes until tender. Drain and let cool.
2. Slice the octopus into bite-sized pieces and place in a bowl.
3. Add olive oil, lemon juice, garlic, parsley, salt, and pepper. Toss to combine.
4. Serve chilled or at room temperature.

Available at Publix, Whole Foods, Target, and Costco.

The whole process with color photos

Baked Trout with Herbs and Almonds

Nutritional Information (per serving):

○ **2** servings

🕐 **10** minutes

Calories:	350 kcal
Protein:	32 g
Fats:	22 g
Carbs:	5 g

Ingredients:

- 2 trout fillets
- 2 tbsp olive oil
- 2 tbsp sliced almonds
- 1 tbsp fresh dill, chopped
- 1 garlic clove, minced
- juice of 1 lemon
- salt and pepper to taste

NB Elegant and Flavorful: Perfect for a special occasion or a weeknight dinner.

Instructions:

1 Preheat the oven to 375°F (190°C).

2 Place the trout fillets on a baking sheet and drizzle with olive oil and lemon juice.

3 Sprinkle with almonds, dill, garlic, salt, and pepper.

4 Bake for 15–20 minutes until the fish is cooked through and the almonds are toasted.

🛒 *Available at Publix, Whole Foods, Target, and Costco.*

The whole process with color photos

Grilled Calamari with Lemon and Garlic

Nutritional Information (per serving):

Calories:	200 kcal
Protein:	25 g
Fats:	10 g
Carbs:	3 g

Ingredients:

- ½ lb calamari, cleaned and cut into rings
- 1 tbsp olive oil
- 2 garlic cloves, minced
- juice of 1 lemon
- fresh parsley for garnish
- salt and pepper to taste

servings 2

minutes 10

NB Light and Healthy: A simple and fresh dish that's ideal for summer grilling.

Instructions:

1 Preheat the grill to medium-high heat.

2 Toss the calamari with olive oil, garlic, salt, and pepper.

3 Grill the calamari for 2–3 minutes on each side until tender.

4 Drizzle with lemon juice and garnish with parsley before serving.

Available at Publix, Whole Foods, Target, and Costco.

The whole process with color photos

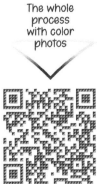

CHAPTER 9:

POULTRY AND MEAT MAINS:

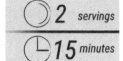

2 servings
15 minutes

Chicken Souvlaki with Tzatziki

Nutritional Information (per serving):

Ingredients:

Calories:	350 kcal
Protein:	30 g
Fats:	15 g
Carbs:	5 g

NB Family-Friendly: This is a great dish for family meals or outdoor grilling.

- 2 chicken breasts, cut into 1-inch cubes
- 2 tbsp olive oil
- juice of 1 lemon
- 2 garlic cloves, minced
- 1 tbsp fresh oregano, chopped
- salt and pepper to taste

For the Tzatziki:
- ½ cup Greek yogurt
- 1 small cucumber, grated and squeezed to remove excess water
- 1 garlic clove, minced
- 1 tbsp fresh dill, chopped
- juice of ½ lemon
- salt and pepper to taste

Instructions:

1. In a bowl, combine the olive oil, lemon juice, garlic, oregano, salt, and pepper. Add the chicken cubes and toss to coat. Marinate for at least 30 minutes, preferably 1 hour.
2. Thread the marinated chicken onto skewers. Preheat the grill or grill pan over medium-high heat.
3. Grill the chicken for 10–15 minutes, turning occasionally, until fully cooked and slightly charred.
4. Meanwhile, make the Tzatziki by mixing all the ingredients in a bowl. Adjust seasoning to taste.
5. Serve the chicken skewers with Tzatziki sauce on the side.

 Available at Publix, Whole Foods, Target, and Costco.

The whole process with color photos

Roasted Chicken with Lemon and Rosemary

Nutritional Information (per serving):

Calories:	400 kcal
Protein:	30 g
Fats:	25 g
Carbs:	2 g

Ingredients:

- 2 bone-in, skin-on chicken thighs
- 1 tbsp olive oil
- juice of 1 lemon
- 2 garlic cloves, minced
- 2 sprigs fresh rosemary
- salt and pepper to taste

servings **2**

minutes **10**

NB Perfect for Weeknights: A simple yet flavorful recipe that's great for a quick dinner.

Instructions:

1. Preheat the oven to 400°F (200°C).
2. Rub the chicken thighs with olive oil, lemon juice, garlic, rosemary, salt, and pepper.
3. Place the chicken in a baking dish and roast for 35–40 minutes, until the skin is crispy and the chicken is cooked through.
4. Let rest for 5 minutes before serving.

Available at Publix, Whole Foods, Target, and Costco.

The whole process with color photos

Lamb Meatballs with Mint and Feta

Nutritional Information (per serving):

◐ 2 servings

🕐 15 minutes

Calories:	450 kcal
Protein:	25 g
Fats:	30 g
Carbs:	10 g

NB Great for Entertaining: These meatballs are perfect as a main dish or appetizer at gatherings.

Ingredients:

- ¹/₂ lb ground lamb
- 1 garlic clove, minced
- 1 tbsp fresh mint, chopped
- ¹/₄ cup crumbled feta cheese
- 1 egg
- ¹/₄ cup breadcrumbs
- salt and pepper to taste
- 1 tbsp olive oil

Instructions:

1 In a bowl, mix together the lamb, garlic, mint, feta, egg, breadcrumbs, salt, and pepper. Form into small meatballs.

2 Heat olive oil in a skillet over medium heat. Add the meatballs and cook for 10–12 minutes, turning occasionally, until browned and cooked through.

3 Serve with a drizzle of olive oil or a side of Tzatziki sauce.

 Available at Publix, Whole Foods, Target, and Costco.

The whole process with color photos

Mediterranean Chicken Stew with Olives

**Nutritional Information
(per serving):**

Calories:	400 kcal
Protein:	35 g
Fats:	20 g
Carbs:	15 g

NB Comforting and Hearty: This stew is perfect for cooler days or when you need a warming meal.

Ingredients:

- 2 chicken thighs, bone-in, skinless
- 1 tbsp olive oil
- 1 small onion, diced
- 2 garlic cloves, minced
- 1 can (15 oz) diced tomatoes
- ½ cup Kalamata olives, pitted and sliced
- 1 tsp dried oregano
- salt and pepper to taste

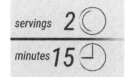

servings 2
minutes 15

Instructions:

1 Heat olive oil in a pot over medium heat. Add the chicken thighs and brown on both sides, about 5 minutes per side. Remove and set aside.

2 In the same pot, sauté the onion and garlic for 5 minutes. Add the diced tomatoes, olives, oregano, salt, and pepper.

3 Return the chicken to the pot, cover, and simmer for 30 minutes until the chicken is cooked through and tender.

4 Serve hot with a garnish of fresh herbs if desired.

Available at Publix, Whole Foods, Target, and Costco.

The whole process with color photos

Grilled Lamb Chops with Garlic and Thyme

Nutritional Information (per serving):

2 servings

10 minutes

Calories:	500 kcal
Protein:	30 g
Fats:	35 g
Carbs:	3 g

Ingredients:

- 4 lamb chops
- 1 tbsp olive oil
- 2 garlic cloves, minced
- 1 tbsp fresh thyme, chopped
- juice of ½ lemon
- salt and pepper to taste

NB Perfect for Special Occasions: An elegant and delicious dish, perfect for dinner parties or date night.

Instructions:

1 Rub the lamb chops with olive oil, garlic, thyme, lemon juice, salt, and pepper.

2 Preheat a grill or grill pan to medium-high heat. Grill the lamb chops for 3–4 minutes on each side for medium-rare.

3 Let the lamb rest for 5 minutes before serving.

Available at Publix, Whole Foods, Target, and Costco.

The whole process with color photos

Chicken Tagine with Apricots and Almonds

**Nutritional Information
(per serving):**

Calories:	450 kcal
Protein:	30 g
Fats:	18 g
Carbs:	35 g

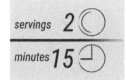

servings 2

minutes 15

Ingredients:

- 2 chicken thighs, bone-in, skinless
- 1 tbsp olive oil
- 1 small onion, diced
- 2 garlic cloves, minced
- ¹/₂ cup dried apricots, chopped
- 1 tbsp honey
- 1 tsp ground cinnamon
- 1 tsp ground cumin
- ¹/₄ cup slivered almonds, toasted
- salt and pepper to taste

NB Exotic and Flavorful: A great dish for those looking to explore the flavors of North Africa.

Instructions:

1. Heat olive oil in a tagine or heavy-bottomed pot over medium heat. Brown the chicken thighs on both sides, then set aside.
2. In the same pot, sauté the onion and garlic for 5 minutes. Add the apricots, honey, cinnamon, cumin, salt, and pepper.
3. Return the chicken to the pot, cover, and simmer for 40 minutes until the chicken is tender and the flavors have melded.
4. Garnish with toasted almonds before serving.

Available at Publix, Whole Foods, Target, and Costco.

The whole process with color photos

Turkey Meatballs with Zucchini and Feta

Nutritional Information (per serving):

2 servings

15 minutes

Calories:	300 kcal
Protein:	30 g
Fats:	15 g
Carbs:	10 g

NB Healthy and Flavorful: A lighter alternative to traditional meatballs, packed with veggies.

Ingredients:

- ¹/₂ lb ground turkey
- 1 small zucchini, grated and squeezed to remove excess water
- ¹/₄ cup crumbled feta cheese
- 1 garlic clove, minced
- 1 egg
- ¹/₄ cup breadcrumbs
- salt and pepper to taste
- 1 tbsp olive oil

Instructions:

1 In a bowl, mix together the turkey, zucchini, feta, garlic, egg, breadcrumbs, salt, and pepper. Form into meatballs.

2 Heat olive oil in a skillet over medium heat. Cook the meatballs for 10–12 minutes, turning occasionally, until browned and cooked through.

3 Serve with a dipping sauce or over a salad.

Available at Publix, Whole Foods, Target, and Costco.

The whole process with color photos

Beef Kebabs with Tzatziki Sauce

Nutritional Information (per serving):

Calories:	320 kcal
Protein:	32 g
Fats:	15 g
Carbs:	7 g

NB Family-Friendly: Great for summer cookouts or family dinners. Low-Carb Option: Perfect for those following a low-carb or ketogenic diet.

Ingredients:

- 1 lb beef sirloin, cut into 1-inch cubes
- 1 red bell pepper, cut into large pieces
- 1 yellow bell pepper, cut into large pieces
- 1 red onion, cut into wedges
- 2 tbsp olive oil
- 1 tbsp lemon juice
- 1 tsp dried oregano
- 1 tsp garlic powder
- salt and pepper, to taste
- 8 wooden skewers (soaked in water for 30 minutes)

servings **4**

minutes **25**

For the Tzatziki Sauce:
- 1 cup Greek yogurt
- 1 cucumber, grated and squeezed of excess water
- 2 cloves garlic, minced
- 1 tbsp lemon juice
- 1 tbsp olive oil
- 1 tbsp fresh dill, chopped
- salt and pepper, to taste

Instructions:

1 *Marinate the Beef:* In a bowl, mix the olive oil, lemon juice, oregano, garlic powder, salt, and pepper. Add the beef cubes and toss to coat. Cover and marinate in the refrigerator for at least 30 minutes.

2 *Prepare the Tzatziki Sauce:* In a separate bowl, mix the Greek yogurt, grated cucumber, garlic, lemon juice, olive oil, dill, salt, and pepper. Refrigerate until ready to serve.

3 *Assemble the Kebabs:* Thread the beef cubes, bell peppers, and onion onto the soaked skewers.

4 *Grill the Kebabs:* Preheat your grill to medium-high heat. Grill the skewers for 8-10 minutes, turning occasionally, until the beef is cooked to your desired doneness.

5 *Serve:* Serve the kebabs with the prepared tzatziki sauce.

Available at Publix, Whole Foods, Target, and Costco.

The whole process with color photos

Pork Tenderloin with Herb Marinade

Nutritional Information (per serving):

◯ **4** servings

🕐 **10** minutes
+1 hour
marinating time

Calories:	240 kcal
Protein:	30 g
Fats:	12 g
Carbs:	2 g

Ingredients:

- 1 lb pork tenderloin
- 2 tbsp olive oil
- 2 tbsp lemon juice
- 2 garlic cloves, minced
- 1 tbsp fresh rosemary, chopped
- 1 tbsp fresh thyme, chopped
- salt and pepper, to taste

NB Perfect for Date Night: This elegant dish is ideal for a romantic dinner.
Make-Ahead: The pork can be marinated ahead of time, making it perfect for meal prep.

Instructions:

1 *Marinate the Pork:* In a bowl, mix olive oil, lemon juice, garlic, rosemary, thyme, salt, and pepper. Add the pork tenderloin and rub the marinade all over. Cover and refrigerate for 1 hour (or overnight for more flavor).

2 *Preheat the Oven:* Preheat your oven to 375°F (190°C).
Sear the Pork: Heat a skillet over medium-high heat. Sear the pork tenderloin on all sides until browned, about 2-3 minutes per side.

3 *Roast the Pork:* Transfer the seared pork to a baking dish and roast in the oven for 20-25 minutes or until the internal temperature reaches 145°F (63°C).

4 *Rest and Serve:* Let the pork rest for 5 minutes before slicing. Serve with a fresh herb garnish.

🛒 *Available at Publix, Whole Foods, Target, and Costco.*

The whole process with color photos

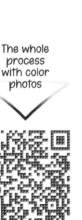

Greek-Style Chicken Wraps with Yogurt Sauce

Nutritional Information (per serving):

Calories: 390 kcal
Protein: 30 g
Fats: 12 g
Carbs: 40 g

Ingredients:

- 2 chicken breasts, grilled and sliced
- 4 whole-wheat pita breads
- 1 cup mixed lettuce leaves
- 1 tomato, sliced
- 1 cucumber, sliced
- 1 small red onion, sliced

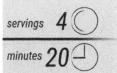

servings 4
minutes 20

NB Family-Friendly: Great for a casual lunch or dinner. Low-Calorie Option: A healthy, satisfying wrap perfect for weight-conscious eaters.

For the Yogurt Sauce:

- 1 cup Greek yogurt
- 1 garlic clove, minced
- 1 tbsp lemon juice
- 1 tbsp fresh dill, chopped
- salt and pepper, to taste

Instructions:

1. **Prepare the Yogurt Sauce:** In a small bowl, mix the Greek yogurt, garlic, lemon juice, dill, salt, and pepper. Set aside.
2. **Assemble the Wraps:** Lay the pita bread on a flat surface. Spread a layer of the yogurt sauce onto each pita. Add the sliced grilled chicken, lettuce, tomato, cucumber, red onion, and crumbled feta.
3. **Wrap and Serve:** Roll up the pita wraps and serve immediately with a side of extra yogurt sauce for dipping.

Available at Publix, Whole Foods, Target, and Costco.

The whole process with color photos

CHAPTER 10:

4 servings

15 minutes

PASTA AND PIZZA

Spaghetti Aglio e Olio (Garlic and Olive Oil)

Nutritional Information (per serving):

Calories:	380 kcal
Protein:	10 g
Fats:	18 g
Carbs:	45 g

Ingredients:

- 12 oz spaghetti
- 1/4 cup extra virgin olive oil
- 6 garlic cloves, thinly sliced
- 1/2 tsp red pepper flakes (optional)
- salt and pepper, to taste
- 1/4 cup fresh parsley, chopped
- freshly grated Parmesan cheese (optional)

NB Quick and Easy: This is a simple, classic pasta dish that takes under 20 minutes to prepare, perfect for a weeknight dinner.

Instructions:

1 *Cook the Spaghetti:* Bring a large pot of salted water to a boil. Cook the spaghetti according to the package instructions until al dente. Drain and set aside, reserving 1/2 cup of pasta water.

2 *Prepare the Garlic Oil:* In a large skillet, heat the olive oil over medium heat. Add the garlic slices and red pepper flakes (if using) and sauté until the garlic is golden and fragrant, about 2 minutes.

3 *Toss the Pasta:* Add the cooked spaghetti to the skillet, tossing to coat in the garlic oil. Add the reserved pasta water a little at a time to create a smooth sauce. Season with salt and pepper.

4 *Serve:* Toss with fresh parsley and sprinkle with Parmesan cheese if desired. Serve immediately.

Available at Publix, Whole Foods, Target, and Costco.

The whole process with color photos

Pesto Pasta with Cherry Tomatoes

Nutritional Information (per serving):

Calories:	450 kcal
Protein:	14 g
Fats:	22 g
Carbs:	50 g

Ingredients:

- 12 oz pasta of your choice (penne or fusilli works well)
- 1 cup cherry tomatoes, halved
- 1 cup fresh basil pesto (store-bought or homemade)
- $^{1}/_{4}$ cup Parmesan cheese, grated
- salt and pepper, to taste
- tbsp olive oil

servings 4

minutes 20

NB Vibrant and Fresh: This dish is perfect for summer, highlighting fresh basil pesto and juicy cherry tomatoes.

Instructions:

1. **Cook the Pasta:** Boil a pot of salted water and cook the pasta according to package instructions. Drain and set aside.
2. **Combine Ingredients:** In a large bowl, toss the hot pasta with the fresh pesto, cherry tomatoes, olive oil, salt, and pepper. Stir until the pasta is fully coated.
3. **Serve:** Top with grated Parmesan and serve warm or at room temperature.

Available at Publix, Whole Foods, Target, and Costco.

The whole process with color photos

Mediterranean Lasagna with Eggplant and Ricotta

6 servings

1 hour

Nutritional Information (per serving):

Calories: 480 kcal
Protein: 22 g
Fats: 22 g
Carbs: 50 g

NB Vegetarian-Friendly:
This lasagna features
Mediterranean flavors with
layers of eggplant, ricotta,
and marinara sauce.

Ingredients:

- 1 large eggplant, thinly sliced
- 9 lasagna noodles (whole wheat if desired)
- 2 cups marinara sauce
- 1½ cups ricotta cheese
- 1 egg, beaten
- 1½ cups shredded mozzarella cheese
- 1 tsp dried oregano
- salt and pepper, to taste
- 2 tbsp olive oil

Instructions:

1 *Prepare the Eggplant:* Preheat the oven to 375°F (190°C). Brush the eggplant slices with olive oil and roast on a baking sheet for 20 minutes, flipping halfway.

2 *Cook the Lasagna Noodles:* Boil the lasagna noodles according to the package directions. Drain and set aside.

3 *Prepare the Ricotta Mixture:* In a bowl, mix the ricotta cheese, egg, oregano, salt, and pepper.

4 *Assemble the Lasagna:* In a greased baking dish, layer marinara sauce, lasagna noodles, roasted eggplant, ricotta mixture, and mozzarella cheese. Repeat layers, finishing with mozzarella cheese on top.

5 *Bake:* Cover with foil and bake for 30 minutes. Remove the foil and bake for an additional 10 minutes until the cheese is golden and bubbly.

6 *Serve:* Let cool for 5 minutes before slicing and serving.

Available at Publix, Whole Foods, Target, and Costco.

The whole
process
with color
photos

Penne Arrabbiata (Spicy Tomato Sauce)

**Nutritional Information
(per serving):**

Calories:	380 kcal
Protein:	10 g
Fats:	15 g
Carbs:	50 g

Ingredients:

- 12 oz penne pasta
- 3 tbsp olive oil
- 4 garlic cloves, minced
- 1 tsp red pepper flakes (adjust to taste)
- 1 can (14 oz) crushed tomatoes
- salt and pepper, to taste
- ¼ cup fresh basil, chopped
- parmesan cheese, for serving

NB Spicy Option: This dish packs heat from red pepper flakes, making it a bold and flavorful pasta choice.

servings	4
minutes	25

Instructions:

1 **Cook the Penne:** Boil the pasta in salted water until al dente. Drain and set aside.

2 **Prepare the Sauce:** In a large skillet, heat the olive oil over medium heat. Add the garlic and red pepper flakes, sautéing for 1 minute. Add the crushed tomatoes and simmer for 15 minutes.

3 Season with salt and pepper.

4 Combine the Pasta: Toss the cooked penne in the sauce and stir to coat.

5 **Serve:** Garnish with fresh basil and Parmesan cheese.

Available at Publix, Whole Foods, Target, and Costco.

The whole process with color photos

Fettuccine with Lemon and Spinach

Nutritional Information (per serving):

4 servings

20 minutes

Calories:	350 kcal
Protein:	10 g
Fats:	12 g
Carbs:	50 g

Ingredients:
- 12 oz fettuccine
- 2 tbsp olive oil
- 2 garlic cloves, minced
- 2 cups fresh spinach
- zest and juice of 1 lemon
- salt and pepper, to taste
- parmesan cheese, for serving

NB Light and Fresh: This pasta dish is light, with fresh lemon and spinach adding a burst of flavor and nutrients.

Instructions:
1. **Cook the Fettuccine:** Boil the pasta in salted water until al dente. Drain, reserving ¼ cup of pasta water.
2. **Sauté the Spinach:** In a skillet, heat olive oil over medium heat. Add the garlic and sauté for 1 minute. Add the spinach and cook until wilted, about 3 minutes.
3. **Combine Ingredients:** Toss the cooked fettuccine with the spinach, lemon zest, lemon juice, and reserved pasta water. Season with salt and pepper.
4. **Serve:** Top with Parmesan cheese and serve immediately.

Available at Publix, Whole Foods, Target, and Costco.

The whole process with color photos

Mediterranean Pizza with Olives and Feta

Nutritional Information (per serving):

Calories:	380 kcal
Protein:	14 g
Fats:	18 g
Carbs:	38 g

NB Vegetarian-Friendly: A delicious Mediterranean-style pizza that combines the salty goodness of olives with creamy feta cheese.

Ingredients:

- 1 pre-made pizza dough (whole wheat or regular)
- 1/2 cup marinara sauce
- 1 cup shredded mozzarella cheese
- 1/2 cup crumbled feta cheese
- 1/4 cup Kalamata olives, pitted and sliced
- 1/2 small red onion, thinly sliced
- 1 tbsp olive oil
- fresh basil leaves, for garnish

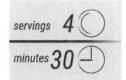

servings **4**

minutes **30**

Instructions:

1 *Preheat the Oven:* Preheat your oven to 475°F (245°C).

2 *Prepare the Dough:* Roll out the pizza dough on a lightly floured surface to your desired thickness. Transfer to a baking sheet or pizza stone.

3 *Assemble the Pizza:* Spread the marinara sauce evenly over the dough. Sprinkle with mozzarella cheese, followed by feta cheese, olives, and red onion slices.

4 *Bake the Pizza:* Drizzle olive oil over the top and bake for 12-15 minutes or until the crust is golden and the cheese is bubbling.

5 *Garnish and Serve:* Remove from the oven, garnish with fresh basil leaves, and serve hot.

Available at Publix, Whole Foods, Target, and Costco.

The whole process with color photos

Greek Flatbread with Kalamata Olives

Nutritional Information (per serving):

4 servings

25 minutes

Calories:	320 kcal
Protein:	10 g
Fats:	16 g
Carbs:	35 g

NB Quick and Easy: This simple flatbread is a great appetizer or light meal, packed with the flavors of the Mediterranean.

Ingredients:

- 4 small flatbreads or pita breads
- ¹/₂ cup Kalamata olives, pitted and chopped
- 1 cup crumbled feta cheese
- 1 tbsp olive oil
- 1 tbsp fresh oregano, chopped
- 1 garlic clove, minced
- ¹/₂ tsp red pepper flakes (optional)
- fresh parsley, for garnish

Instructions:

1. **Preheat the Oven:** Preheat the oven to 400°F (200°C).
2. **Prepare the Flatbread:** Arrange the flatbreads on a baking sheet. Brush each flatbread with olive oil.
3. **Add Toppings:** Sprinkle the minced garlic evenly over the flatbreads. Top with chopped Kalamata olives, crumbled feta, oregano, and red pepper flakes.
4. **Bake:** Bake in the oven for 10 minutes, or until the edges of the flatbreads are golden and crispy.
5. **Garnish and Serve:** Remove from the oven, garnish with fresh parsley, and serve immediately.

Available at Publix, Whole Foods, Trader Joe's, and Costco.

The whole process with color photos

Shrimp Pasta with Lemon and Capers

Nutritional Information (per serving):

Calories:	420 kcal
Protein:	28 g
Fats:	12 g
Carbs:	50 g

NB Light and Flavorful: This shrimp pasta has bright flavors from lemon and capers, making it a refreshing yet hearty dish.

Ingredients:

- 12 oz linguine or spaghetti
- 1 lb shrimp, peeled and deveined
- 2 tbsp olive oil
- 2 garlic cloves, minced
- 2 tbsp capers, drained
- zest and juice of 1 lemon
- ¹/₄ cup white wine (optional)
- salt and pepper, to taste
- fresh parsley, chopped, for garnish

servings **4**
minutes **20**

Instructions:

1 *Cook the Pasta:* Boil a large pot of salted water and cook the pasta until al dente. Drain, reserving ¼ cup of pasta water.

2 *Cook the Shrimp:* In a large skillet, heat olive oil over medium heat. Add the shrimp and cook for 2-3 minutes on each side until pink. Remove from the skillet and set aside.

3 *Prepare the Sauce:* In the same skillet, add garlic and sauté for 1 minute. Add capers, lemon zest, lemon juice, and white wine (if using). Cook for 2 minutes, allowing the sauce to reduce slightly.

4 *Combine:* Add the pasta and shrimp back into the skillet and toss to coat. Use the reserved pasta water to loosen the sauce if needed. Season with salt and pepper.

5 *Serve:* Garnish with chopped parsley and serve immediately.

Available at Publix, Whole Foods, Trader Joe's, and Costco.

The whole process with color photos

Spinach and Ricotta Ravioli

Nutritional Information (per serving):

🌓 **4** servings

🕐 **35** minutes
(+30 minutes for resting dough, if homemade)

Calories:	460 kcal
Protein:	18 g
Fats:	22 g
Carbs:	50 g

NB Comforting and Creamy: These homemade ravioli are filled with creamy ricotta and fresh spinach, making for a perfect indulgence.

Ingredients:

- 2 cups fresh spinach, chopped
- 1 cup ricotta cheese
- $1/4$ cup Parmesan cheese, grated
- 1 egg yolk
- 1 garlic clove, minced
- salt and pepper, to taste
- fresh pasta dough (store-bought or homemade)
- 2 tbsp butter
- 1 tbsp olive oil
- fresh basil, for garnish

Instructions:

1. **Prepare the Filling:** In a skillet, sauté the garlic and spinach in olive oil until wilted. Let it cool slightly, then mix with ricotta, Parmesan, egg yolk, salt, and pepper in a bowl.
2. **Assemble the Ravioli:** Roll out the pasta dough and cut into small squares. Place a spoonful of the spinach mixture onto half of the squares, then cover with the remaining squares. Press the edges with a fork to seal.
3. **Cook the Ravioli:** Boil salted water and cook the ravioli for 3-4 minutes, or until they float to the surface. Drain gently.
4. **Prepare the Sauce:** In a skillet, melt butter and olive oil over medium heat. Toss the cooked ravioli in the butter sauce for 1-2 minutes.
5. **Serve:** Garnish with fresh basil and serve with extra Parmesan cheese.

🛒 *Available at Publix, Whole Foods, Trader Joe's, and Costco.*

The whole process with color photos

Whole-Wheat Pasta with Artichokes and Lemon

Nutritional Information (per serving):

Calories:	400 kcal
Protein:	16 g
Fats:	14 g
Carbs:	50 g

Ingredients:

- 12 oz whole-wheat pasta
- 1 can (14 oz) artichoke hearts, drained and quartered
- 2 tbsp olive oil
- 2 garlic cloves, minced
- 2 zest and juice of 1 lemon
- salt and pepper, to taste
- ¹/₂ cup Parmesan cheese, grated
  fresh parsley, chopped, for garnish

servings 4
minutes 30

NB Healthy and Light: whole-wheat pasta pairs beautifully with tender artichokes and a refreshing lemon sauce.

Instructions:

1 *Cook the Pasta:* Boil a large pot of salted water and cook the pasta according to package instructions. Drain and set aside.

2 *Sauté the Artichokes:* In a large skillet, heat olive oil over medium heat. Add garlic and sauté for 1 minute. Add the artichokes and cook for 3-4 minutes until lightly browned.

3 *Combine Ingredients:* Add the cooked pasta to the skillet along with lemon zest, lemon juice, and Parmesan cheese. Toss to combine. Season with salt and pepper.

4 *Serve:* Garnish with fresh parsley and serve with additional Parmesan cheese.

Available at Publix, Whole Foods, Trader Joe's, and Costco.

The whole process with color photos

CHAPTER 11:

DESSERTS & SWEETS

⊘ **24**servings

🕐 **1** hour

Baklava with Honey and Pistachios

Nutritional Information (per serving):

Calories:	250 kcal
Protein:	3 g
Fats:	16 g
Carbs:	25 g

Ingredients:

- 1 package filo dough (16 oz), thawed
- 1 1/2 cups pistachios, chopped
- 1 cup unsalted butter, melted
- 1 cup honey
- 1/2 cup sugar
- 1 tsp cinnamon
- 1/2 tsp ground cloves

NB Traditional Mediterranean Dessert: Flaky, sweet, and rich, this dessert is perfect for special occasions.

Instructions:

1 **Preheat the Oven:** Preheat your oven to 350°F (175°C).

2 **Prepare the Nut Mixture:** In a bowl, combine the chopped pistachios, sugar, cinnamon, and ground cloves.

3 **Layer the Filo Dough:** Brush a 9x13-inch baking dish with melted butter. Layer 10 sheets of filo dough, brushing each with butter. Spread a layer of the nut mixture over the dough. Repeat with the remaining dough and nut mixture, finishing with a top layer of 10 buttered filo sheets.

4 **Cut and Bake:** Using a sharp knife, cut the baklava into small squares or diamond shapes. Bake for 45 minutes, until golden and crisp.

5 **Make the Syrup:** While the baklava bakes, heat honey in a small saucepan over low heat until warm. Drizzle the warm honey over the hot baklava once it's out of the oven.

6 **Cool and Serve:** Allow the baklava to cool completely before serving.

 Available at Trader Joe's, Whole Foods, and local Middle Eastern markets.

The whole process with color photos

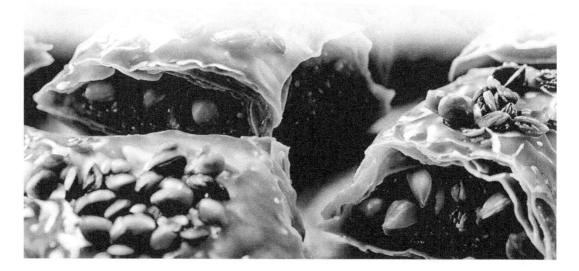

Olive Oil Cake with Citrus Zest

Nutritional Information (per serving):

Calories:	320 kcal
Protein:	5 g
Fats:	12 g
Carbs:	45 g

NB Light and Moist: This cake has a delicate flavor from the olive oil and bright citrus zest.

Ingredients:

- 1³/₄ cups all-purpose flour
- 1 cup sugar
- ¹/₂ cup extra virgin olive oil
- 3 large eggs
- zest of 1 lemon and 1 orange
- ¹/₂ cup fresh orange juice
- 1 tsp baking powder
- ¹/₂ tsp baking soda
- 1/4 tsp salt
- powdered sugar, for dusting

servings **8**

hour **1**

Instructions:

1 *Preheat the Oven:* Preheat the oven to 350°F (175°C). Grease a 9-inch round cake pan.

2 *Mix Wet Ingredients:* In a large bowl, whisk together the olive oil, sugar, eggs, citrus zest, and orange juice.

3 *Add Dry Ingredients:* In another bowl, whisk together the flour, baking powder, baking soda, and salt. Gradually add the dry ingredients to the wet ingredients, stirring until just combined.

4 *Bake:* Pour the batter into the prepared pan and bake for 40-45 minutes, or until a toothpick inserted into the center comes out clean.

5 *Cool and Serve:* Let the cake cool completely, then dust with powdered sugar before serving.

Available at Whole Foods, Trader Joe's, and most local supermarkets.

The whole process with color photos

Yogurt with Fresh Berries and Almonds.

**Nutritional Information
(per serving):**

○ **2** servings

🕐 **10** minutes

Calories:	200 kcal
Protein:	10 g
Fats:	7 g
Carbs:	25 g

NB Gluten-Free, Rich in Antioxidants

Ingredients:

— 1 cup plain Greek yogurt
— ¹/₂ cup fresh mixed berries
   (strawberries, blueberries, raspberries)
— 2 tbsp sliced almonds
— 1 tbsp honey
— ¹/₂ tsp vanilla extract (optional)

Instructions:

1 Divide Greek yogurt evenly into two bowls.
   Top each bowl with fresh mixed berries and sliced almonds.
2 Drizzle with honey and add a touch of vanilla extract if desired.
3 Serve immediately for a fresh and flavorful dessert.

🛒 *Available at Trader Joe's, Whole Foods, and local grocery stores.*

The whole process with color photos

Orange and Almond Cake

Nutritional Information (per serving):

Calories: 350 kcal
Protein: 10 g
Fats: 20 g
Carbs: 35 g

NB Gluten-Free: This cake is made with almond flour, offering a rich, nutty flavor.

Ingredients:

- 2 large oranges
- 6 large eggs
- 1¼ cups almond flour
- 1 cup sugar
- 1 tsp baking powder
- 1 tsp vanilla extract
- powdered sugar, for dusting

servings **8**

hour **1**

Instructions:

1. **Cook the Oranges:** Boil the oranges in a pot of water for 1 hour, then drain and cool. Once cooled, blend the oranges (with peel) into a smooth puree.
2. **Preheat the Oven:** Preheat the oven to 350°F (175°C). Grease a 9-inch round cake pan.
3. **Mix Wet Ingredients:** In a large bowl, beat the eggs and sugar until light and fluffy. Stir in the orange puree and vanilla extract.
4. **Add Dry Ingredients:** Fold in the almond flour and baking powder until well combined.
5. **Bake:** Pour the batter into the prepared pan and bake for 45-50 minutes or until a toothpick comes out clean.
6. **Cool and Serve:** Let the cake cool, then dust with powdered sugar before serving.

Available at Trader Joe's, Whole Foods, and health food stores.

The whole process with color photos

Figs Poached in Red Wine

**Nutritional Information
(per serving):**

○ **4** *servings*

◔ **25** *minutes*

Calories:	*180 kcal*
Protein:	*1 g*
Fats:	*0 g*
Carbs:	*35 g*

Ingredients:
- 12 fresh figs
- 1 1/2 cups red wine
- 1/4 cup honey
- 1 cinnamon stick
- 1 star anise
- 1 tsp orange zest

NB Elegant Dessert: A deliciously simple and sophisticated dessert with rich Mediterranean flavors.

Instructions:

1 *Prepare the Poaching Liquid:* In a saucepan, combine red wine, honey, cinnamon stick, star anise, and orange zest. Bring to a simmer over medium heat.

2 *Poach the Figs:* Add the figs to the liquid and poach for 10-12 minutes, turning occasionally, until soft but still holding their shape.

3 *Serve:* Remove the figs and reduce the liquid until slightly thickened. Serve the figs with a drizzle of the poaching syrup.

🛒 *Available at Whole Foods, Trader Joe's, and local grocery stores.*

The whole process with color photos

Rosewater Cookies

Nutritional Information (per serving):

Calories:	120 kcal
Protein:	2 g
Fats:	8 g
Carbs:	12 g

Ingredients:

- 1 cup unsalted butter, softened
- ½ cup powdered sugar
- 1 tsp rosewater
- 1¾ cups all-purpose flour
- ½ cup ground pistachios
- extra powdered sugar for dusting

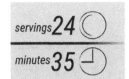

servings 24

minutes 35

Delicate and Fragrant: These cookies combine the rich flavor of pistachios with the subtle aroma of rosewater.

Instructions:

1. **Preheat the Oven:** Preheat the oven to 350°F (175°C). Line a baking sheet with parchment paper.
2. **Cream the Butter and Sugar:** In a large bowl, cream the butter and powdered sugar until light and fluffy. Stir in the rosewater.
3. **Add the Flour and Pistachios:** Gradually add the flour and ground pistachios, mixing until just combined.
4. **Shape the Cookies:** Roll the dough into small balls and place on the prepared baking sheet. Flatten slightly with your palm.
5. **Bake:** Bake for 12-15 minutes, or until the edges are lightly golden.
6. **Dust and Serve:** Let the cookies cool, then dust with extra powdered sugar before serving.

Available at Whole Foods, Trader Joe's, and local gourmet stores.

The whole process with color photos

Fresh Fruit Salad with Mint

Nutritional Information (per serving):

4 servings

15 minutes

Calories:	120 kcal
Protein:	1 g
Fats:	0 g
Carbs:	30 g

Ingredients:

- 2 cups strawberries, hulled and halved
- 1 cup blueberries
- 1 cup diced pineapple
- 2 kiwis, peeled and sliced
- 1 orange, peeled and segmented
- 2 tbsp fresh mint, chopped
- 1 tbsp honey
- juice of 1 lemon

NB Refreshing and Healthy: A light, refreshing dessert with a mix of seasonal fruits and a hint of mint.

Instructions:

1 **Prepare the Fruit:** In a large bowl, combine the strawberries, blueberries, pineapple, kiwi, and orange segments.

3 **Add the Dressing:** In a small bowl, whisk together the honey and lemon juice. Drizzle the mixture over the fruit.

Toss with Mint: Gently toss the fruit with the chopped mint to evenly coat with the dressing.

4 **Serve:** Serve immediately or chill in the refrigerator for 30 minutes before serving.

 Available at most grocery stores, including Whole Foods and Trader Joe's.

The whole process with color photos

Honey and Sesame Bars (Pasteli)

Nutritional Information (per serving):

Calories:	100 kcal
Protein:	2 g
Fats:	7 g
Carbs:	9 g

Ingredients:

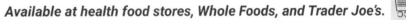

- 1 cup sesame seeds
- ½ cup honey

bars **12**

minutes **10**
+2 hours to set

NB Traditional Greek Treat: A simple and nutritious snack made with just two ingredients—sesame seeds and honey.

Instructions:

1 **Toast the Sesame Seeds:** In a dry skillet, toast the sesame seeds over medium heat for 3-4 minutes until golden and fragrant.

2 **Heat the Honey:** In a small saucepan, warm the honey over medium heat for about 5 minutes, stirring constantly until it reaches a thicker consistency.

3 **Combine:** Stir the toasted sesame seeds into the honey and mix well.

4 **Set:** Pour the mixture into a parchment-lined 8x8-inch baking dish and press down firmly to create an even layer. Allow it to cool and set for about 2 hours at room temperature or in the refrigerator.

5 **Slice and Serve:** Once set, slice into bars and serve.

Available at health food stores, Whole Foods, and Trader Joe's.

The whole process with color photos

Ricotta Cheesecake with Lemon

Nutritional Information (per serving):

○ **8** servings

🕐 **1**₁₅ hour minutes

Calories:	280 kcal
Protein:	8 g
Fats:	18 g
Carbs:	22 g

Ingredients:

- 1½ cups ricotta cheese
- 8 oz cream cheese, softened
- ½ cup sugar
- 3 large eggs
- zest of 2 lemons
- 1 tsp vanilla extract
- 1 tbsp all-purpose flour
- 1 prepared graham cracker crust (9-inch)

NB Light and Creamy: A lighter twist on traditional cheesecake, made with ricotta and brightened with lemon zest.

Instructions:

1. **Preheat the Oven:** Preheat the oven to 325°F (160°C).
2. **Mix the Filling:** In a large bowl, beat together the ricotta, cream cheese, and sugar until smooth. Add the eggs one at a time, beating well after each addition. Stir in the lemon zest, vanilla extract, and flour until combined.
3. **Pour into Crust:** Pour the cheesecake mixture into the prepared graham cracker crust.
4. **Bake:** Bake for 45-50 minutes, or until the center is set and the edges are lightly golden. Turn off the oven and let the cheesecake cool in the oven with the door slightly open for 1 hour.
5. **Chill and Serve:** Transfer to the refrigerator to chill for at least 4 hours or overnight before serving.

🛒 *Available at most grocery stores, including Whole Foods and Trader Joe's.*

The whole process with color photos

Almond and Date Energy Bites

Nutritional Information (per serving):

Calories:	120 kcal
Protein:	3 g
Fats:	7 g
Carbs:	14 g

Ingredients:

- 1 cup almonds
- 1 cup Medjool dates, pitted
- 2 tbsp unsweetened cocoa powder
- 1 tbsp coconut oil
- 1 tsp vanilla extract
- ¼ cup shredded coconut (optional, for rolling)

bites 12

minutes 10

NB No-Bake and Nutrient-Dense: These energy bites are perfect for a quick snack or dessert, providing a natural source of energy.

Instructions:

1. **Blend the Ingredients:** In a food processor, blend the almonds until finely ground. Add the dates, cocoa powder, coconut oil, and vanilla extract. Blend until the mixture forms a sticky dough.
2. **Form the Bites:** Scoop out tablespoon-sized portions of the mixture and roll into balls. If desired, roll the bites in shredded coconut to coat.
3. **Chill and Serve:** Place the energy bites on a plate and refrigerate for at least 30 minutes before serving.

Available at most grocery stores, including Whole Foods and Trader Joe's.

The whole process with color photos

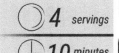 118

CHAPTER 12:

DRINKS AND SMOOTHIES

⏱ 4 servings
⏱ 10 minutes

Pomegranate and Mint Juice

Nutritional Information (per serving):

		Ingredients:
		2 cups pomegranate seeds (about 2 pomegranates)
Calories:	60 kcal	2 cups water
Protein:	1 g	1 tbsp honey (optional)
Fats:	0 g	2 tbsp fresh mint leaves
Carbs:	15 g	ice cubes

NB Refreshing Antioxidant Boost: A vibrant juice packed with antioxidants, perfect for a refreshing, healthy start to the day.

Instructions:

1 *Blend the Pomegranate:* Place the pomegranate seeds and water in a blender. Blend on high for 1-2 minutes until the seeds are broken down and the juice is smooth.

2 *Strain:* Strain the mixture through a fine mesh sieve into a pitcher to remove the seeds.

3 *Sweeten and Add Mint:* Stir in the honey (if using) and mint leaves. Let it chill for 10 minutes for the mint flavor to infuse.

4 *Serve:* Pour over ice and serve cold.

🛒 *Available at most grocery stores, including Whole Foods and Trader Joe's.*

The whole process with color photos

Iced Green Tea with Citrus

Nutritional Information (per serving):

Calories:	20 kcal
Protein:	0 g
Fats:	0 g
Carbs:	5 g

Ingredients:

- 4 green tea bags
- 4 cups water
- juice of 2 lemons
- juice of 1 orange
- 1 tbsp honey (optional)
- ice cubes
- lemon and orange slices for garnish

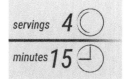

servings 4
minutes 15

NB Refreshing and Revitalizing: A perfect summer drink combining the health benefits of green tea and citrus.

Instructions:

1 *Brew the Green Tea:* Boil the water and steep the green tea bags for 3-5 minutes. Remove the tea bags and let the tea cool to room temperature.

2 *Add Citrus and Sweetener:* Stir in the lemon juice, orange juice, and honey (if using).

3 *Chill and Serve:* Pour the tea over ice and garnish with lemon and orange slices.

Available at most grocery stores, including Whole Foods and Trader Joe's.

The whole process with color photos

Mediterranean Sangria

**Nutritional Information
(per serving):**

⊘ **6** servings

⊕ **15** minutes
+1 hour
chilling
time

Calories: 150 kcal
Protein: 0 g
Fats: 0 g
Carbs: 12 g

Ingredients:

—1 bottle (750 ml) dry red wine
—1 orange, sliced
—1 lemon, sliced
—1 lime, sliced
—1 cup fresh berries (strawberries, blueberries, or raspberries)
—$^1/_4$ cup brandy
—2 tbsp honey
—2 cups sparkling water

NB Perfect for Gatherings:
A fruity Mediterranean twist
on classic sangria, featuring a
mix of fresh fruits and wine.

Instructions:

1 *Prepare the Fruit:* In a large pitcher, combine the sliced orange, lemon, lime, and berries.
2 *Mix the Sangria:* Add the red wine, brandy, and honey to the pitcher. Stir to combine.
3 *Chill:* Let the sangria chill in the refrigerator for at least 1 hour to allow the flavors to meld.
4 *Serve:* Just before serving, stir in the sparkling water. Serve over ice.

🛒 *Available at most grocery stores, including Whole Foods and Trader Joe's.*

The whole
process
with color
photos

Cucumber Mint Smoothie

**Nutritional Information
(per serving):**

Calories:	90 kcal
Protein:	7 g
Fats:	3 g
Carbs:	10 g

Ingredients:

- 1 cucumber, peeled and chopped
- 1 cup Greek yogurt
- ¼ cup fresh mint leaves
- juice of 1 lemon
- 1 tbsp honey
- ice cubes

servings **2**

minutes **10**

 Cooling and Hydrating: A light and refreshing smoothie perfect for hot days.

Instructions:

1 **Blend the Ingredients:** Place the cucumber, Greek yogurt, mint leaves, lemon juice, and honey in a blender. Blend until smooth.

2 **Serve:** Pour into glasses and serve cold over ice.

Available at most grocery stores, including Whole Foods and Trader Joe's.

The whole process with color photos

Lemon and Basil Infused Water

**Nutritional Information
(per serving):**

4 servings	
5 minutes	

Calories:	5 kcal
Protein:	0 g
Fats:	0 g
Carbs:	1 g

Ingredients:

- 1 lemon, thinly sliced
- ¼ cup fresh basil leaves
- 4 cups water
- ice cubes

NB Refreshing and Simple: A perfect way to stay hydrated with a burst of flavor from fresh lemon and basil.

Instructions:

1 *Prepare the Ingredients:* In a large pitcher, combine the lemon slices and basil leaves.

2 *Infuse the Water:* Add the water and ice cubes. Let sit for 10-15 minutes to allow the flavors to infuse.

3 *Serve:* Pour into glasses and enjoy throughout the day.

Available at most grocery stores, including Whole Foods and Trader Joe's.

The whole process with color photos

Greek Frappe Coffee

**Nutritional Information
(per serving):**

		Ingredients:
		2 tsp instant coffee
Calories:	20 kcal	1 tsp sugar (optional)
Protein:	0 g	¼ cup cold water
Fats:	0 g	ice cubes
Carbs:	5 g	cold milk or water to fill

serving	1
minutes	5

NB Classic Greek Coffee: A frothy and refreshing coffee drink perfect for hot days.

Instructions:

1 **Froth the Coffee:** In a shaker or jar with a tight-fitting lid, combine the instant coffee, sugar, and cold water. Shake vigorously until frothy.

2 **Serve:** Pour the frothy coffee into a tall glass filled with ice. Add cold milk or water to fill the glass.

3 **Stir and Enjoy:** Stir before drinking and enjoy your refreshing frappe.

Available at most grocery stores, including Whole Foods and Trader Joe's.

The whole process with color photos

Spiced Moroccan Tea

Nutritional Information (per serving):

🕐 4 servings		
🕐 10 minutes	Calories:	30 kcal
	Protein:	0 g
	Fats:	0 g
	Carbs:	7 g

Ingredients:

- 4 cups water
- 4 green tea bags
- ¼ cup fresh mint leaves
- 1 cinnamon stick
- 2 tbsp sugar or honey (optional)

 Aromatic and Soothing: A traditional Moroccan tea with a mix of fresh mint and spices.

Instructions:

1 Boil the Water: Bring the water to a boil and add the green tea bags, fresh mint, cinnamon stick, and sugar (if using).

2 Steep and Serve: Allow the tea to steep for 5 minutes. Remove the tea bags and cinnamon stick before serving.

🛒 *Available at most grocery stores, including Whole Foods and Trader Joe's.*

The whole process with color photos

Fresh Orange Juice with Ginger

Nutritional Information (per serving):

Calories:	120 kcal
Protein:	2 g
Fats:	0 g
Carbs:	28 g

Ingredients:

- 6 large oranges, juiced
- 1 -inch piece of fresh ginger, peeled and grated
- ice cubes

serving **4**

minutes **10**

NB Immune-Boosting: A zesty twist on fresh orange juice with the addition of ginger for extra flavor and health benefits.

Instructions:

1. **Juice the Oranges:** Juice the oranges and strain into a pitcher.
2. **Add the Ginger:** Stir in the grated ginger and let sit for 5 minutes to infuse.
3. **Serve:** Serve over ice for a refreshing start to the day.

Available at most grocery stores, including Whole Foods and Trader Joe's.

The whole process with color photos

Watermelon and Mint Smoothie

Nutritional Information (per serving):

	2 servings
	10 minutes

Calories:	80 kcal
Protein:	4 g
Fats:	1 g
Carbs:	16 g

Ingredients:

- 2 cups watermelon, cubed and chilled
- ½ cup Greek yogurt
- 1 tbsp fresh mint leaves
- juice of 1 lime
- ice cubes

NB Hydrating and Refreshing: A cooling and delicious smoothie perfect for summer.

Instructions:

1 **Blend the Ingredients:** Combine the watermelon, Greek yogurt, mint leaves, lime juice, and ice cubes in a blender. Blend until smooth.

2 **Serve:** Pour into glasses and enjoy immediately.

Available at most grocery stores, including Whole Foods and Trader Joe's.

The whole process with color photos

Almond and Date Smoothie

**Nutritional Information
(per serving):**

Calories:	180 kcal
Protein:	7 g
Fats:	8 g
Carbs:	22 g

Ingredients:

- 1 cup almond milk
- 1/2 cup Greek yogurt
- 4 medjool dates, pitted
- 1 tbsp almond butter
- 1/2 tsp cinnamon
- ice cubes

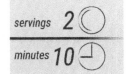

servings 2

minutes 10

 Energy Boosting: A rich and creamy smoothie packed with natural sweetness and protein.

Instructions:

1 *Blend the Ingredients:* Place all the ingredients in a blender and blend until smooth.

2 *Serve:* Pour into glasses and serve chilled.

Available at most grocery stores, including Whole Foods and Trader Joe's.

The whole process with color photos

CHAPTER 13:

SAUCES, DRESSINGS, DIPS

4 servings

5 minutes

Lemon Tahini Sauce

Nutritional Information (per serving):

Calories:	150 kcal
Protein:	4 g
Fats:	12 g
Carbs:	5 g

Ingredients:

- ¹/₂ cup tahini
- ¹/₄ cup lemon juice
- ¹/₄ cup water
- 1 garlic clove, minced
- 1 tbsp olive oil
- salt to taste

 NB Versatile and Creamy: This sauce is perfect for drizzling over salads, roasted vegetables, or grilled meats.

Instructions:

1 *Mix the Ingredients:* In a medium bowl, whisk together tahini, lemon juice, water, minced garlic, and olive oil until smooth.

2 *Adjust Consistency:* Add more water if needed to reach your desired consistency.

3 *Season:* Add salt to taste.

Available at most grocery stores, including Whole Foods and Trader Joe's.

The whole process with color photos

Garlic Yogurt Sauce

Nutritional Information (per serving):

Calories:	80 kcal
Protein:	6 g
Fats:	4 g
Carbs:	3 g

Ingredients:

- 1 cup Greek yogurt
- 1 garlic clove, minced
- 1 tbsp lemon juice
- 1 tbsp olive oil
- salt and pepper to taste

serving	4
minutes	5

NB Cooling and Creamy: Ideal for kebabs, falafel, or as a dip for vegetables.

Instructions:

1 **Combine the Ingredients:** In a bowl, mix Greek yogurt, minced garlic, lemon juice, and olive oil.

2 **Season:** Add salt and pepper to taste.

3 **Serve Chilled:** Serve as a dip or drizzle.

Available at most grocery stores, including Whole Foods and Trader Joe's.

The whole process with color photos

Basil Pesto

Nutritional Information (per serving):

○ **4** servings

⏱ **10** minutes

Calories:	200 kcal
Protein:	4 g
Fats:	20 g
Carbs:	2 g

Ingredients:
- 2 cups fresh basil leaves
- ¼ cup pine nuts
- ½ cup grated Parmesan cheese
- ½ cup olive oil
- 2 garlic cloves, minced
- salt to taste

NB Rich and Flavorful: Great for pasta, pizza, or as a sandwich spread.

Instructions:

1. **Blend the Ingredients:** In a food processor, combine basil leaves, pine nuts, Parmesan cheese, garlic, and salt.
2. **Add Olive Oil:** While blending, slowly pour in the olive oil until the mixture is smooth.
3. **Store and Serve:** Use immediately or store in the refrigerator for up to one week.

🛒 **Available at most grocery stores, including Whole Foods and Trader Joe's.**

The whole process with color photos

Harissa Paste

Nutritional Information (per serving):

Calories:	50 kcal
Protein:	1 g
Fats:	4 g
Carbs:	3 g

Ingredients:

- 3 dried red chilies, soaked
- 1 tbsp tomato paste
- 1 tsp cumin seeds
- 1 tsp coriander seeds
- 2 garlic cloves
- 2 tbsp olive oil
- salt to taste

serving **4**

minutes **10**

 Spicy and Smoky: Use as a marinade or condiment for a kick of North African flavor.

Instructions:

1. **Toast the Spices:** Toast cumin and coriander seeds in a dry pan for 1-2 minutes until fragrant.
2. **Blend:** Blend the soaked chilies, toasted spices, garlic, tomato paste, olive oil, and salt into a smooth paste.
3. **Store:** Store in a jar and refrigerate for up to two weeks.

Available at most grocery stores, including Whole Foods and Trader Joe's. Specialty spice shops may have unique dried chilies and seeds.

The whole process with color photos

Classic Vinaigrette with Olive Oil and Lemon

4 servings

5 minutes

Nutritional Information (per serving):

Calories:	90 kcal
Protein:	0 g
Fats:	9 g
Carbs:	1 g

Ingredients:

- ¹/₄ cup olive oil
- 2 tbsp lemon juice
- 1 tsp Dijon mustard
- salt and pepper to taste

NB Light and Tangy: A go-to dressing for salads or grilled vegetables.

Instructions:

1 *Whisk the Ingredients:* In a small bowl, whisk together olive oil, lemon juice, Dijon mustard, salt, and pepper.

2 *Adjust Seasoning:* Adjust seasoning to taste and serve immediately.

Available at most grocery stores, including Whole Foods and Trader Joe's.

The whole process with color photos

Tzatziki Sauce

**Nutritional Information
(per serving):**

Calories:	70 kcal
Protein:	5 g
Fats:	4 g
Carbs:	3 g

Ingredients:

- 1 cup Greek yogurt
- 1 cucumber, grated and squeezed to remove excess water
- 1 garlic clove, minced
- 1 tbsp lemon juice
- 1 tbsp olive oil
- 2 tbsp fresh dill, chopped
- salt to taste

serving 4

minutes 10

NB Cooling and Refreshing: Perfect for grilled meats or as a dip.

Instructions:

1 **Combine the Ingredients:** In a bowl, mix Greek yogurt, grated cucumber, garlic, lemon juice, olive oil, and dill.

2 **Season:** Add salt to taste and refrigerate for at least 30 minutes before serving.

Available at most grocery stores, including Whole Foods and Trader Joe's.

The whole process with color photos

Roasted Red Pepper Sauce

Nutritional Information (per serving):

○ **4** servings

🕐 **10** minutes

Calories:	80 kcal
Protein:	1 g
Fats:	7 g
Carbs:	4 g

Ingredients:

- 2 roasted red peppers, peeled and chopped
- 2 garlic cloves, minced
- 2 tbsp olive oil
- 1 tsp smoked paprika
- salt and pepper to taste

 NB Smoky and Sweet: A great sauce for pasta or grilled vegetables.

Instructions:

1 *Blend the Ingredients:* In a food processor, blend roasted red peppers, garlic, olive oil, smoked paprika, salt, and pepper until smooth.

2 *Store and Serve:* Store in the refrigerator and use as a sauce for pasta or roasted vegetables.

🛒 *Available at most grocery stores, including Whole Foods and Trader Joe's.*

The whole process with color photos

Garlic and Herb Butter

Nutritional Information (per serving):

Calories:	100 kcal
Protein:	0 g
Fats:	11 g
Carbs:	0 g

Ingredients:

- ½ cup unsalted butter, softened
- 2 garlic cloves, minced
- 1 tbsp fresh parsley, chopped
- 1 tbsp fresh thyme, chopped
- salt to taste

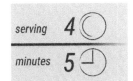

serving 4
minutes 5

NB Rich and Versatile: Perfect for spreading on bread or topping grilled meats and vegetables.

Instructions:

1. **Mix the Ingredients:** In a bowl, mix softened butter, minced garlic, parsley, thyme, and salt until well combined.
2. **Store:** Refrigerate for up to one week or freeze for longer storage.

Available at most grocery stores, including Whole Foods and Trader Joe's.

The whole process with color photos

Muhammara (Roasted Pepper and Walnut Dip)

Nutritional Information (per serving):

◐ **4** servings

🕐 **15** minutes

Calories: 120 kcal
Protein: 3 g
Fats: 10 g
Carbs: 7 g

Ingredients:

- 2 roasted red peppers, peeled and chopped
- ½ cup walnuts
- 1 garlic clove, minced
- 1 tsp cumin
- 1 tbsp pomegranate molasses
- 2 tbsp olive oil
- salt to taste

NB Rich and Nutty: A smoky and slightly sweet dip from the Levant region.

Instructions:

1. **Blend the Ingredients:** In a food processor, blend roasted peppers, walnuts, garlic, cumin, pomegranate molasses, olive oil, and salt until smooth.
2. **Serve:** Serve with pita bread or vegetables.

 Available at most grocery stores, including Whole Foods and Trader Joe's. Specialty stores may offer pomegranate molasses.

The whole process with color photos

Tapenade (Olive and Caper Spread)

Nutritional Information (per serving):

Calories:	90 kcal
Protein:	1 g
Fats:	9 g
Carbs:	2 g

Ingredients:
- 1 cup Kalamata olives, pitted
- 1 tbsp capers, drained
- 2 garlic cloves
- 2 tbsp olive oil
- 1 tsp lemon juice

serving **4**

minutes **10**

 NB Salty and Savory: A great spread for bread or a topping for grilled meats.

Instructions:

1 *Blend the Ingredients:* In a food processor, blend Kalamata olives, capers, garlic, olive oil, and lemon juice until smooth.

2 *Serve:* Serve as a spread for bread or with grilled meats.

Available at most grocery stores, including Whole Foods and Trader Joe's.

The whole process with color photos

CHAPTER 14:

PERSONALIZED HEALTH JOURNAL

The Mediterranean diet is more than just a way of eating—it's a lifestyle that emphasizes long-term well-being and balance. To support you on this journey, we've created a *Personalized Health Journal* designed to help you track your progress, plan your meals, and stay motivated as you embrace the Mediterranean way of life. This journal will guide you in reflecting on your health and well-being, ensuring that you stay on course and make the most of your Mediterranean diet experience.

SIMPLE TEMPLATES FOR DAILY, WEEKLY, AND MONTHLY REFLECTION

To make tracking your progress simple and intuitive, the personalized health journal provides structured templates for daily, weekly, and monthly monitoring. This way, you can easily observe your improvements, adjust your approach as necessary, and stay motivated to achieve your health goals.

DAILY TRACKING

Each day, you'll have sections to record important aspects of your Mediterranean diet journey:

Meals: Log your meals for breakfast, lunch, dinner, and snacks. This will help you stay on track and see how your food choices align with Mediterranean diet principles.

Calories, Proteins, Fats, and Carbs: Track your macronutrient intake to ensure you're balancing your consumption of healthy fats, lean proteins, and complex carbohydrates from fruits, vegetables, and whole grains.

Energy Levels and Mood: Make note of how your energy and mood fluctuate throughout the day. Tracking this can help identify which meals provide sustained energy and enhance well-being.

Water Intake: Hydration is a key part of a healthy lifestyle. Log your daily water intake to ensure you're drinking enough, particularly with meals rich in vegetables and olive oil.

Personal Notes: Jot down any reflections, cravings, or challenges you face during the day. This space allows for personal insights and adjustments as you progress through the diet.

WEEKLY TRACKING

At the end of each week, take time to reflect on your progress with the following sections:

Goals and Progress: Set small, actionable goals for each week—whether it's trying a new Mediterranean recipe, increasing your vegetable intake, or including more fish in your meals. Reflect on your success at the end of the week.

Weight and Measurements: If you're monitoring weight or body measurements, this section allows you to track physical changes and see the results of your healthy eating habits.

Well-being Reflection: Assess your overall well-being, including energy levels, mood, digestion, and sleep quality. This holistic reflection can help you fine-tune your meal plan.

Challenges and Adjustments: Record any challenges you faced, such as eating out or managing cravings, and brainstorm solutions or adjustments for the following week.

MONTHLY SUMMARY

Every month, you'll be able to review your overall progress and accomplishments with a detailed summary section:

Achievements: Celebrate the milestones you've reached—whether it's improved energy, better digestion, or hitting a weight goal. Recognizing these successes keeps you motivated.

Adjustments: Reflect on what worked and where changes are needed. Perhaps you want to incorporate more physical activity or try new Mediterranean recipes. This is where you plan for the next month.

New Goals: Set new monthly goals based on your reflections and progress. These goals should continue to build upon the foundation of the Mediterranean diet—such as increasing your intake of healthy fats or reducing processed foods.

TIPS FOR SETTING AND ACHIEVING HEALTH GOALS

Achieving success with the Mediterranean diet is not just about following a meal plan—it's about setting realistic and achievable goals to support long-term health. Here are some tips to make the most of your health journal:

Set Specific Goals: Instead of vague objectives like "eat healthier," create specific goals such as "incorporate three servings of vegetables at every meal" or "cook fish twice a week."

Be Flexible: It's important to listen to your body. If something isn't working, adjust your goals. For example, if you're finding it hard to eat whole grains, try introducing them gradually or experimenting with different types like farro or barley.

Celebrate Every Victory: Small achievements lead to big results. Whether you've managed to cut down on processed foods or feel more energized, take pride in every step forward.

ADJUSTING YOUR ROUTINE FOR OPTIMAL RESULTS

The Mediterranean diet emphasizes balance and variety, and as you progress, it's important to adjust your routine to match your evolving needs. Use your journal to reflect on what's working and what isn't, and make the following adjustments as needed:

If energy levels dip, consider increasing your intake of healthy fats such as olive oil or nuts.

If cravings arise, focus on nutrient-dense snacks like hummus with veggies or Greek yogurt with honey and nuts to stay satisfied.

If weight loss or maintenance is a goal, review portion sizes and experiment with lightening meals by adding more greens and cutting back on refined carbs.

MOTIVATION AND TIPS

To keep you inspired and focused on your health goals, the journal is sprinkled with motivational quotes and practical tips. Whether you need advice on meal prepping or a reminder of the health benefits of the Mediterranean diet, these sections will serve as helpful guidance throughout your journey.

By regularly using this personalized health journal, you'll be able to build a complete picture of your Mediterranean diet experience. Whether you're just starting or continuing your journey, tracking your progress will ensure that you stay motivated, adaptable, and, most importantly, successful in achieving long-term health.

CHAPTER 15:

THE MEDITERRANEAN DIET: ORIGINS, QUALITY, AND SUSTAINABILITY

The Mediterranean diet has a rich history that dates back centuries and spans several countries across the Mediterranean region, including Greece, Italy, Spain, and parts of the Middle East. This chapter explores the roots of the Mediterranean diet, its core values of quality and sustainability, and how these principles contribute to the overall health benefits associated with this way of eating.

ORIGINS OF THE MEDITERRANEAN DIET

The Mediterranean diet reflects the traditional cooking styles of countries that border the Mediterranean Sea. Historically, these communities relied heavily on locally grown and seasonal foods, such as fruits, vegetables, whole grains, legumes, and olive oil. Fresh seafood was also abundant, and meat was typically consumed in smaller portions, with a focus on lean sources like poultry and fish.

Staples of the Mediterranean diet include:

Olive Oil: Often called "liquid gold" by ancient civilizations, olive oil is a cornerstone of the Mediterranean diet. It's rich in monounsaturated fats, which support heart health.

Fresh Produce: The Mediterranean diet emphasizes eating seasonal, fresh fruits and vegetables, many of which are known for their antioxidant and anti-inflammatory properties.

Whole Grains and Legumes: Grains like barley, farro, and wheat, as well as legumes such as lentils and chickpeas, provide essential fiber and protein.

Seafood: Fish, especially oily fish like sardines, mackerel, and salmon, are consumed regularly and provide omega-3 fatty acids.

Moderate Dairy: Cheese and yogurt are consumed in moderation, often serving as accompaniments to meals rather than the main focus.

QUALITY INGREDIENTS: THE HEART OF MEDITERRANEAN CUISINE

In Mediterranean cooking, the emphasis is placed on using the highest quality ingredients possible. The diet champions the use of fresh, local, and organic products whenever available. This not only enhances flavor but also ensures the nutritional value of the food is preserved.

Key ingredients to look for when shopping for a Mediterranean diet include:

Extra Virgin Olive Oil: Always opt for extra virgin olive oil over processed alternatives. Look for cold-pressed oils that are rich in polyphenols.

Wild-Caught Seafood: Choose sustainably sourced, wild-caught fish to get the maximum benefit from omega-3 fats and avoid harmful chemicals often found in farm-raised fish.

Whole Grains: Look for whole grains like bulgur, farro, quinoa, and whole wheat products.

Fresh Herbs: Mediterranean cooking relies heavily on fresh herbs like basil, oregano, rosemary, thyme, and mint for flavoring dishes.

SUSTAINABILITY AND ENVIRONMENTAL IMPACT

The Mediterranean diet is not only good for your health, but it's also good for the planet. It emphasizes locally grown, seasonal foods, which supports regional farmers and reduces the carbon footprint associated with transporting food long distances. The diet also favors plant-based meals and minimal processing, further contributing to its sustainability.

Key principles of sustainability in the Mediterranean diet include:

Seasonality: Eating fruits and vegetables that are in season not only maximizes nutritional value but also minimizes the environmental impact of food production.

Less Meat, More Plants: A focus on plant-based meals reduces the demand for resource-intensive animal farming, which can be harmful to the environment.

Minimal Food Waste: Mediterranean cooking often incorporates leftovers into new meals, reducing food waste and making the most of what's available.

HOW TO SOURCE HIGH-QUALITY, SUSTAINABLE INGREDIENTS

Sourcing high-quality ingredients is crucial for following the Mediterranean diet. When shopping, consider the following tips:

Farmers' Markets: Support local farmers by purchasing fresh, seasonal produce from farmers' markets.

Sustainable Seafood: Look for seafood labeled as sustainably caught or certified by organizations like the Marine Stewardship Council (MSC).

Organic Options: Whenever possible, choose organic produce to avoid harmful pesticides and support environmentally friendly farming practices.

Ethically Sourced Meat: If you eat meat, opt for grass-fed, pasture-raised, or organic options that prioritize animal welfare and environmental sustainability.

CONCLUSION

A FINAL WORD ON SUSTAINING A MEDITERRANEAN LIFESTYLE

The Mediterranean diet is more than just a way of eating—it's a lifestyle that promotes balance, wellness, and enjoyment of food. It encourages mindful eating, savoring each meal, and sharing food with loved ones, all while promoting a healthy, sustainable way of life.

As you've discovered throughout this book, the Mediterranean diet is rich in health benefits, from heart health and weight management to reducing inflammation and boosting longevity. But it's also flexible and adaptable, making it easy to incorporate into your daily routine, no matter where you live or what your dietary preferences may be.

TIPS FOR MAINTAINING BALANCE IN DIET AND LIFE

Embrace Whole Foods: Focus on fresh, unprocessed foods, and try to prepare meals from scratch as often as possible.

Eat Mindfully: Pay attention to portion sizes, eat slowly, and savor the flavors of your meals.

Stay Active: Regular physical activity is an important part of the Mediterranean lifestyle. Try incorporating daily walks, gardening, or yoga into your routine.

Socialize Around Food: Share meals with family and friends whenever possible, as food is meant to bring people together.

ENCOURAGEMENT FOR LONG-TERM HEALTH SUCCESS

Achieving long-term health success with the Mediterranean diet involves making gradual, sustainable changes to your eating habits. Remember, it's not about following strict rules—it's about enjoying the process of eating well, exploring new flavors, and finding joy in nourishing your body.

Keep in mind that setbacks may occur along the way, but the key to success is consistency. Stick with the principles of the Mediterranean diet, stay flexible, and continue to learn about new ways to improve your health.

WHERE TO GO FROM HERE: FURTHER RESOURCES AND COMMUNITIES

To continue your Mediterranean journey, consider joining online communities, forums, or local groups focused on Mediterranean cooking and wellness. You'll find endless inspiration, support, and new ideas for keeping your meals exciting and nutritious.

For additional resources, here are a few recommendations:

Books: Explore other cookbooks, food guides, and wellness books that dive deeper into Mediterranean culture and cuisine.

Podcasts: Tune in to health and wellness podcasts that feature experts discussing the benefits of the Mediterranean diet.

Websites: Visit reputable websites dedicated to Mediterranean cooking for more recipe ideas, health tips, and expert advice.

Remember, adopting the Mediterranean lifestyle is not about perfection. It's about making meaningful changes that improve your well-being over time. The journey is just as important as the destination—so enjoy every step!

Made in United States
North Haven, CT
11 January 2025

64296283R00083